Kathryn
Kuhlman

Kathryn Kuhlman

The life she led, the legacy she left

HELEN KOOIMAN HOSIER

Fleming H. Revell Company
Old Tappan, New Jersey

Library of Congress Cataloging in Publication Data

Hosier, Helen Kooiman.
    Kathyrn Kuhlman.
    Includes bibliographical references.
    1. Kuhlman, Kathryn.
BV3785.K8467   269'.2'0924 [B]   76-18277
ISBN 0-8007-0827-X
ISBN 0-8007-0826-1 pbk.

TO
honor the memory of
Kathryn Kuhlman
who so honored the Lord
during her lifetime

TO
those who loved her so very much
and
whose lives were touched by the hand of God
ministering through His handmaiden, Kathryn Kuhlman

Contents

Preface

A BOOK LIKE THIS could never have come into being without the interest and help of many individuals. From the very outset, this was a combined effort on the part of dozens of people, each willing to go out of his or her way to do whatever was necessary to put together material that would bring honor to the memory of Kathryn Kuhlman.

I had the feeling, over and over again, as letters, pictures, and telephone calls came, and trips were made, that Miss Kuhlman herself would have been deeply moved by the interest and efforts of these people. It was amazing to us the way material arrived right at the very moment when I particularly needed it (and this happened day after day). I felt a supernatural direction and power hovering over the entire undertaking. Many of the people who cooperated said they felt this same direction urging them to send material and offer insights. There were times when I felt that Kathryn was peeking over my shoulder when, late at night and on into the early hours of the morning, I'd be working on the manuscript. Sometimes she'd be laughing, other times modestly objecting, at some points protesting (but only mildly), and most often just encouraging me on as she saw that God was being given the glory and the credit even as she always insisted on doing during her lifetime.

I must tell you also that I experienced what David Wilkerson described so beautifully in chapter 11, which Kathryn described as the Holy Spirit in us as a "quickening Spirit" (Romans 8:11).

So then, to those wonderful people who have endeared themselves to me, I offer my deepest appreciation: Alfred Schlapper, Homer Perry, Gary L. Beissenherz, Rudi Plaut, "Buddy" Samuels, Dora Flandermeyer, Edna Tebbenkamp, and Ralph Erdwin, all of Concordia, Missouri (Kathryn's hometown); Mr. Roland Petering, and Mrs. Edna (Pape) Sargent of Kansas City, Missouri, and Mrs. Fern (Kroencke)

Cullom, Lexington, Missouri, and to the anonymous friend who contributed so much—each of these individuals were childhood friends; Mrs. Freada Planting, Boise, Idaho; Mrs. Marie Sleeper, Caldwell, Idaho; Mr. and Mrs. John Sasenbery, Nampa, Idaho; Jackie Ford, Caldwell, Idaho; Mr. and Mrs. Paul Ferrin, San Jose, California; Mrs. Vonetta Hardy, Denver, Colorado; John Wilkerson, Pacific Grove, California; David Wilkerson, Lindale, Texas; Captain John LeVrier and his wife Sara, and Sue Berkman, Houston, Texas; Jim Reid, chaplain of the Las Vegas Strip, and the Rev. Melvin A. Pekrul, Las Vegas, Nevada; Loraine Geers, Sikeston, Missouri; Jane Jones, Costa Mesa, California; Jean Waltz, Los Angeles, California; Russell Chandler, Los Angeles, California; Dr. Viola Frymann, La Jolla, California; Mr. and Mrs. Wilbur Wacker, Palos Verdes, California; Mr. and Mrs. Robert Atkins, Akron, Ohio. And to any others whom I may have inadvertently omitted, or who helped in ways unknown to the author, please know of my gratitude.

Special thanks to my dear and loyal friends, Ed and Thelma Elfstrom, who were always right there to provide counsel, encouragement, a home away from home, and tender ministrations of love and concern. My husband, Herman, assisted in ways too numerous to mention, but always with patience, honesty and keen discernment; and son, Kraig, "gave up" his mother for seven weeks, but was considerate, interested, and helpful.

My gratitude to other friends who corresponded and assured us of their prayers; and to the Fleming H. Revell Company for entrusting this responsibility to me.

HELEN KOOIMAN HOSIER
April 20, 1976

1
Exit the Scoffing Skeptic

. . . . in the last days there will come scoffers. . . .

2 Peter 3:3

"I THINK SHE's got them hypnotized. . . . Yes, I'm sure that must be it."

My friend, sitting next to me in the Melodyland Christian Center auditorium (Anaheim, California), whispered back, "I think you're right. Seems to me I remember reading something about if you touch a person just right, in a certain place in the neck, you can make them fall over."

We sat on the edge of our seats watching from the rear of the auditorium. We'd decided to sit there so we could get out more easily, "just in case we get bored."

"Isn't this something else?" my friend whispered with obvious disapproval. I agreed even while I was craning my neck to get a better view. To myself I was thinking: *She's right, but still, I wish we'd have sat nearer the front so we could see better.* My friend whispered once more, "Whenever you're ready to go, I'm more than ready."

"Oh, all right," I answered, and we got out of our seats to leave. But even as we left, I was walking partially backwards, trying to get a view of what was happening on the large circular Melodyland stage. I noticed my friend was doing the same, as we kept bumping into each other walking up the aisle to the exit at the rear of the auditorium.

People were falling right and left. Kathryn Kuhlman would reach out her long arms and her hands would touch someone and down they'd go. She'd take a tiny quick step backwards, utter a little *Oh!* and turn her attention to someone else. Ushers were scurrying around trying to catch everyone as fast as they'd go down, but there simply weren't enough ushers. Many people fell without anyone to cushion the fall. Even Ralph Wilkerson, pastor of the church, had gone down. I knew Wilkerson, having visited his church on numerous occasions, and I was shocked to see this big man go down like a feather.

It was a strange sight for eyes unaccustomed to such goings-on and we were both more than a little goggle-eyed.

Now we were out on the street, my friend and I, the dazzling lights of Disneyland across busy Harbor Boulevard to the west greeted us. Nearby, directly north across the street, was the big Grand Hotel. "Let's go over and have a cup of coffee," I suggested.

"Hypnotism. That's it; that's *got* to be it." I was murmuring to myself.

"Of course people don't 'fall under the power' like that today. Where do people get the idea that's real?" Our skepticism gushed forth—two self-righteous know-it-all cynics marching triumphantly through the crosswalk on the busy street separating Melodyland from the hotel parking lot.

"Did you ever see such a show?" My friend threw back her head as she laughed.

"And her entry! What did you think of *that?*" It was my turn to throw in a jab. "Green chiffon, wafting in like an angel. Have you ever seen a green angel with red hair?" I mimicked Kathryn Kuhlman, holding an imaginary fluff of chiffon dress by the hemline, waltzing slightly.

Laughing. Scoffing. We entered the Grand Hotel, poking fun, playing the role to the hilt of enlightened critics, as if we had a perfect right to pass judgment.

Over cups of coffee we continued our assessment of "the show" we had just witnessed.

"Those floodlights beaming on her coming down the aisle! How theatrical can you get!"

"Yes, but what about the way she talks . . . 'Dear *Jeez*-hus, I need you to help me . . . *hell*-p me. . . .' "

I've often reflected on that conversation. And I've often wondered why God didn't strike us dead for such blasphemy! For yes, this was outright contempt, disgusting behavior on our part directed toward one of God's servants. Indeed, one of His *choice* servants.

That scene—or one similar to it—has been repeated times without number over the years, and often, for the most part, I fear, by those who should know better—those who call themselves *Christians.*

Dave Wilkerson, writing in the Foreword of her book, *Nothing Is Impossible with God,* said: "She is loved and admired by millions and maligned only by those who are down on divine healing or who have made no effort at all to understand her or what she stands for. . . ."

A minister of the gospel sat at our dining room table and made the comment, "She's demon-possessed."

Such skepticism and criticism is to be expected from what the Christian world would term "the secular world," but in view of the clear teaching of the Bible, those who name the name Christian are out of step with God's directives when they place themselves in the role of the judge of this universe.

Where did we ever get the idea that *our* way of thinking was necessarily the *right* way and beyond reproach? Or that we had an inside track and could determine the validity of another individual's way of doing things (especially as it relates to matters of a religious nature)?

God began to deal with me about this kind of an attitude in my own life. Certainly He didn't deal with me in the way I deserved! It began with a gnawing doubt in my mind that kept on saying: *But Kathryn Kuhlman didn't touch everyone in the neck.*

An answer came flying back: *You don't necessarily have to touch someone to hypnotize them. It was the power of suggestion. She's psychic.*

The argument continued off and on in my thinking for some time.

Then came the disturbing question: *Who are you, Helen, to think you can tell God how to run the lives of others, particularly those whose mannerisms and methods differ so much from yours?*

I began to feel like I was on the witness stand, having to defend myself in a case that had already been judged. I felt more and more guilty as the inner interrogation continued. *But it was so . . . so overly dramatic . . . so foolish almost. . . .*

But God hath chosen the foolish things of the world to confound the wise.[1]

I winced as the Word of God came rushing to Kathryn Kuhlman's defense. My own mind was turning against me as the words of the Apostle Paul tumbled out:

Judge not, that ye be not judged.[2]

Oh, everybody uses that verse. The Bible also says something about exercising righteous judgment. . . . Yes, Jesus said,

. . . my judgment is just. . . .[3]

Not yours, my dear.

and he shall judge the world in righteousness. . . .[4]

Well, we're to be discerning. Yes, we're supposed to exercise good discernment. . . .

But the natural man receiveth not the things of the Spirit of God: for they are foolishness unto him: neither can he know them, because they are spiritually discerned.[5]

I had cut my teeth, as it were, on the Bible. Bible memorization was as much a part of my growing-up years as eating.

Then I really became defensive. *But God, You know how I was raised. You know how Mama used to say to me when I'd get too inquisitive about things, "That's not the way you were brought up."*

What I was saying to the Lord at this point in the struggle was true. When my questioning mind sought out the whys and wherefores of a given situation, my old-fashioned Dutch mother would remind me of my "bringing up." Somewhere along the line, because we have been taught to honor and obey our parents, and to respect those in authority over us—if we have learned to do this (and I had)—we are caught in the guilt trap and, not wanting to be disloyal, we succumb to silence.

But such retreat can eventually become painful, particularly if one is at all sensitive to that "still, small inner voice."

Now, once again, I was responding, carrying on a conversation with that unseen Presence, and the unspoken voice.

When we are caught in the tumult of conflicting emotions, some of which have their origin in earlier training and teaching, God deals with us patiently, teaching us as we stumble along, ever ready to bring us to new heights of glory and understanding.

Habits and ways of thinking are hard to break, especially as they relate to religious beliefs. Preconceived ideas, formed through the years, rise up to shout at us when we start examining that which is different from all we've lived with and been exposed to up to a certain point.

As I've reread every Kathryn Kuhlman book and media comments about her, I have discovered again and again that a great majority of people began as scoffers when they visited her services. They came out of curiosity as much as anything. They were wary. There was open distrust on the part of some; desperation on the part of countless others; and still others were intensely loyal. There were extremes in reactions, but no one could get away from the fact that something out of the ordinary happened. I could not ignore the inner voice.

I'm not exactly certain when my thinking took a turn for a change. I couldn't tell you the date, time, or place. And it didn't happen as a result of a miraculous healing in my life, or in the life of someone dear to me as happened so often with those who came into a realization that Kathryn Kuhlman was for real and being used in a mighty and miracle-working way by God. But change it did.

I think the roots for change had their origin at that first exposure in person to the ministry of Kathryn Kuhlman. That she was unique I could not deny. That her presence in the auditorium set off a reaction throughout the audience was unmistakable.

Basic honesty, a virtue my mother had also pounded into me with relentless fervor, compelled me to take another look.

When you are honest with God, you can be sure something is going to happen. Answers will be forthcoming. The Bible tells me that God delights in honesty in the inner man. Those whose lives were touched by Kathryn Kuhlman in a most dramatic way would be the first to tell you that they were forced to the conclusion that God honors such open disclosure of one's inner man and He is a rewarder of those who diligently seek the truth.

"Dear God, give me an open mind. Make me more teachable. I want to learn every lesson You have for me, in Your way. Whatever it takes, whomever it takes, I'm ready." With that prayer of release the walls of defensiveness began to crumble, not immediately all at once, but slowly and surely God was working to answer this woman's heart's cry.

For years prior to this I had been selling Kathryn Kuhlman's books in our Christian bookstores. As I listened to the enthusiastic comments from those buying these books, I inwardly cringed. Now I found myself reading them.

Whereas before I was totally turned off to the possibility of anyone's being used like that in our day, now I was able to read and the scales which had so blinded me before seemed to drop off. (None are so blind as those who will *not* see!)

God was answering my prayer.

Kathryn Kuhlman's way of speaking and some of her mannerisms I still found difficulty in accepting, but I *was* watching her television program. "Leave it to Me," God was saying. "I make no two people alike. Kathryn Kuhlman is her own person; you are you. Let *Me* handle it for you."

Convicted I had to confess, "Dear God, who am I to dictate to You how someone else should dress, talk, or act. Forgive me, Father."

And God did just that!

Not only did He forgive and remove the guilt, but then I began to see the beauty of Jesus as the husky voice on TV cried out, "I be . . . leeva in miracles."

Exit the scoffing skeptic.

2

"Someday I Want a Book Written. . . ."

. . . of making many books there is no end. . . .
Ecclesiastes 12:12

"SOMEDAY I want a book written . . ." she paused, reflecting, and the silence that followed was long as she tilted her head back, closed her eyes, and folded her hands to her chest. "Yes, I want a book written." Now her eyes were open, her head came down, and she looked intently at me. "Up until now I did not want it published until after I was gone, because I felt as though if I had it published while I was alive, people would think I did it to get public sympathy—that that would have been my motive. Now I'm not so sure, and I may do it before I die."

The book did not get published before she died. Now she is gone. The book to which Kathryn Kuhlman was alluding in her conversation with me that day would have been autobiographical in content.

There will be many books about her published in the future, both those of a biographical nature and still others pertaining to those who have been touched by God's healing power through the miracle services. Kathryn Kuhlman's comment to me came one year and four days before she died. In the interim, a chapter biography of her life, based on that interview, had been written for inclusion in the third in a series of books I have done on the lives of contemporary Christians.

What was I doing sitting in a room offstage somewhere in the cavernous Shrine Auditorium in Los Angeles? What right had I to suppose I could do justice to the life of Kathryn Kuhlman in a mere chapter biography? These were the questions going through my head as I sat waiting with my husband for Miss Kuhlman to meet with us on February 16, 1975.

From the time I had written her on January 6, 1975, until I received her reply written ten days later, I had some reservations about the

wisdom of my request. Even though I had previously conducted interviews, traveled all over the country, and written many biographical
accounts, still I wondered about the wisdom of my attempting to do
Miss Kuhlman's story. I well knew of the adulation which had been
heaped upon her; I knew also the criticism which existed both in the
media and among some in the Christian world. Was I equal to meeting
the expectations of the former group and the raised eyebrows and
criticisms of the latter? And what of Miss Kuhlman herself? I did not
want to disappoint her nor hurt her ministry in any way. Most of all,
however, I wanted God's leading and His blessing on whatever was
attempted and subsequently written.

God's leading was sought and with it came assurance that I should
contact Kathryn Kuhlman. My letter, written to her, said (in part):

> Our books have been keeping company for years on the shelves of
> Christian booksellers across the country. Now I am hoping we will have
> the opportunity to get to know each other in person and "keep com-
> pany," even if only briefly, sometime soon. [By way of explanation:
> because my books appear under the name of Helen Kooiman and we
> are both *K*'s, they are often on the same bookshelf. Many booksellers
> tell me our names are sometimes confused, and I have been called and
> introduced as Helen Kuhlman more times than I can possibly recall! I
> always feel honored, believe me.]

But it was Kathryn Kuhlman's reply which is of significance, for it
underscores the graciousness which characterized the woman. She
wrote:

> Before I was halfway through reading your beautifully written letter, I
> had decided to make time—either in Los Angeles or Oakland—for your
> interview . . . I will be delighted to meet you as you requested. . . .
> On hearing from you again, I will be happy to arrange a time for
> you. . . .

And now, here I was, waiting for the woman who has been acclaimed as "one of the most extraordinary Christian mystics and clairvoyants of our time. . . . the greatest charismatic healer of our time."[6]

My first reaction to Kathryn Kuhlman's appearance was one of surprise. It had been a long time since I'd seen her at the Melodyland Christian Center, and then not at close range. She was taller than I remembered her to be. Tall. Red-haired. Slender. (Slender or too thin, tired, and maybe not too well?) Those impressions immediately registered.

Time magazine had described her as being joyfully middleclass, fiftyish, a lady who likes fine clothes, and who looks for all the world like dozens of the women in her audience. That magazine article ("Miracle Woman" dated September 14, 1970) somehow had found its way into a folder in my files labeled KATHRYN KUHLMAN.

I had made a mental note of that article. Now I quickly computed another five years to their figure and came up with a number in the late fifties. In all honesty, looking at Kathryn Kuhlman on February 16, 1975, I would have to say I think *Time* misjudged her age.

But age has nothing to do with one's vitality, and Kathryn Kuhlman was a spirited, energetic woman that day, possessing more drive and dynamism than many women in their twenties (even though she did look tired). Louise Farr, a free-lance writer living in Los Angeles, writing in *Ms.* magazine, described her as "an astoundingly energetic woman." One would have to assume that this was her way throughout the years —a woman with a tremendous drive, supernatural energy, and a charisma that was difficult to define.

"She had a sharp eye for detail," said John Wilkerson, pastor of an Assembly of God church in Pacific Grove, California, in a conversation we had following her death. The Wilkersons had been active in some of Kathryn's meetings in Minneapolis a number of years ago. "There wasn't a thing going on in the auditorium, both before, during, and after the meetings, that she wasn't aware of. Oh, she was pernickety," he laughingly explained. "I don't mean this in an uncomplimentary way," he emphasized, "but everything had to go just right at the meetings. That was Kathryn. . . . Before a meeting she'd be back there, behind the platform, controlling and giving orders. She'd look out over the auditorium and if there was a box or a bag, or something in the aisle, she'd spot it. She'd call one of us over and say, 'Go out to the middle aisle, about halfway back and ask that man to put that under his seat. We don't want someone tripping on that thing whatever it is.' "

Confirmation of what John Wilkerson said had actually come from Kathryn Kuhlman herself in our interview. "Sometimes I think I can outwork six men," she told us. "Why, some men come home from work completely exhausted after their eight-hour day. I don't believe I was God's first choice for this kind of work. I've wondered . . . maybe His first choice was a *man* who . . . how shall I word this . . . a *man* who messed things up. Maybe I was . . . I need to say this *exactly* the way I mean it . . . maybe I was just *stoop*-id enough y' know." Anyone who had been in her presence on a one-to-one basis conversationally knows that one of her favorite and oft-used expressions was "Y' know."

She was irrepressibly folksy on or off the platform. Reporters picked up on this implying somehow that it was contrived. More than one writer termed her smile "always beatific," meaning showing happiness or delight. Was this state of blissfulness and joy an act?

That day she continued, "I was one of those people who had no fear of *going* into this kind of ministry because I didn't know what was involved. You've heard of people doing that, haven't you? Y' know, they just go ahead and . . . *do* it! Few people know what a *per*sonal ministry this is; I'm so involved that, literally speaking—yes, I admit—I call *all* the shots."

That did not come across as a put-on act. It struck us both as being downright open and honest.

John Wilkerson who had said she was quite fussy also remembered with warm gratitude her kindness. "So thoughtful," he said. "She was so kind. Any year that I had anything to do at all with her or helping in one of her meetings, that year she'd remember my family and me with a Christmas gift. Can you imagine that?" he questioned. "Think how many people she would have had to remember that way if she was going to be consistent and not single out a favorite few."

I knew that what he was saying was true. We had seen Miss Kuhlman in action ourselves at the Shrine Auditorium that day. Bustling about at a fever pitch, she was cognizant of all that was going on about her. Her awareness was keen, honed by countless numbers of such meetings, yet no meeting ever lost its uniqueness. Each service was special to her, a sacred trust given her by God Himself; she must be responsible, above all, to Him, one sensed.

The Sunday we met her at the Shrine has been indelibly impressed on our memories. She was dressèd in a very plain black gored skirt that swirled over her knees and around her thin legs. Her striped red-and-black full-sleeved blouse accentuated her long arms. She stood with one arm resting on her waist in a hip-out stance, the other hand cupped her chin. The intensity of her blue eyes revealed much as we talked. Eyes, they say, are the mirror of the soul. I liked what I saw in those "mirrors."

A little over a year later, in talking to a former schoolmate of Kathryn's, it was significant to hear her say, "When Kathryn came to Kansas City in 1972 I attended her meeting. Prior to that, knowing that she would be in our city, I had written her suggesting that perhaps we could get together. Kathryn wrote back saying she'd like that. She was the same dramatic Kathryn that I'd always known—she was always dramatic in the way she spoke and acted. She was an actress even in the fifth grade! She had not changed much in looks—red-haired, very slim, stylish, attractive. But the thing I noticed that was different about her was the peculiar expression in her eyes. . . ." Fern Cullom struggled to explain that "peculiar expression."

"Mystical?" I suggested. "In the Spirit?"

"Yes, yes, that's it," she affirmed.

Kathryn would have recognized Fern Cullom as Fern Kroencke from her Concordia, Missouri, days. And Kathryn would have appreciated Fern's comments.

Never once did I feel Kathryn Kuhlman was hedging in answering our questions. Her active mind carefully sought out the right words as she gave forthright replies. She was not deliberately evasive. But she was accustomed to being interviewed; and she had undoubtedly fielded the same questions many times.

There was a quality about her that was unmistakable—and anyone who has interviewed as many people as I have has come to the point where one recognizes certain things—Kathryn Kuhlman was no fanatic, frantic phony.

Dramatic, yes. Phony, no.

If there is one thing that has caused as much speculation among people through the years as their interest in the miraculous and the healings, it has been Kathryn Kuhlman's flair for being so dramatic. And if there is one thing that has made her the subject of criticism—wrongly or rightly—it has been this very thing. "I just couldn't stand to look at her with all those exaggerated actions," I have heard said in one way or another by various individuals.

"She turned me off!" said another of Kathryn's former Concordia friends. "Sure she was always waving her arms and acting even when we were kids, but I wish she'd have outgrown it. She should have been a movie star instead of a woman evangelist."

Even before talking to the residents of Kathryn's hometown I had come to the conclusion that she was not play acting but that this was just Kathryn. Another writer labeled her "a frantic dynamo whose ability to manipulate an audience is in the tradition of all great entertainers."

The visit among her classmates confirmed my conclusion—a conclusion, by the way, which was not arrived at easily. I, too, had great difficulty in sitting through one of her telecasts for some time in my life.

Another thing I struggled with (as did so many others) was her manner of speech. Her speech was always deliberate and slow. "Why do you speak with such deliberateness?" I questioned her.

I knew she'd been asked that before, and I'd read her answer in a book, but I wanted to hear it firsthand.

"I was a stutterer as a little girl. Over and over again my mother would stop me as I talked and say, 'Now, baby, talk slowly.' Even now I have to watch myself very carefully.

"But I was also born in the South, and I was very southern in my speech. I love the southern accent in people, it's beautiful. But I was not always understood and realized this very early in my preaching. I decided to work hard to overcome this and developed the habit of speaking so distinctly that everyone could understand. I would rather speak one sentence very slowly and be understood than say ten thousand words and no one know what I said afterwards."

In discussing Kathryn with Roland Petering of Kansas City (another former resident of Concordia, Missouri, and a neighbor and childhood playmate of Kathryn's), he remarked, "I enjoyed watching Kathryn on television and listening to her. She really must have worked hard on her speech—you know, when she was a kid she had that strong southern accent; we all did. You'd have had to hear her then and now to appreciate the difference."

Now that was another side of the coin! Here was someone who appreciated that slow, deliberate speaking voice, and for good reason— the very reason why Kathryn Kuhlman herself explained over and over that she'd worked to overcome this. Again, it was no phony act; it was a genuine effort and not without price—the costly gift of dedication of herself unreservedly even to a recognition on her part that she had to do something about her speech!

The Shrine service that Sunday, like other such services held in various places throughout the years was well coordinated with consistent emphasis on giving God the glory.

Ann Butler, writing in the "Roto" section of the *Pittsburgh Press,* said that the tone of everything at the services is set "by the preacher's natural flair for showmanship. It will not be solemn, but it won't be an uproar either. Always, it will seem staged, directed, and produced by the media-conscious but ever-sincere Miss Kuhlman."[7]

If honor and praise could accrue to God through the piano artistry of a gifted pianist, then such a person was used; if hearts could be softened to the point of yielding to God through the voice of a talented vocalist, then that individual was asked to be the soloist; if a supernatural healing had taken place at a previous meeting, that person participated by relating what happened. Other critics called the meetings, among other things, "glossy inspirational packages," but Kathryn Kuhlman viewed each service as a responsibility before the Lord—a charge from Him to which she must be faithful. If there was interesting variety, entertainment value in what took place, she was among the first to thank God for dedicated people whose gifts were being used in this way. But entertainment? Not entertainment for entertainment's sake.

3

Concordia! Can Anything Good Come From There?

. . . "We have found the Messiah! . . . His name is Jesus, the
son of Joseph from Nazareth!"
  "Nazareth!" exclaimed Nathanael. "Can anything good
come from there?"

John 1:45, 46

"I WAS SEVENTEEN YEARS OLD when the War Between the States broke
out in April 1861. Yes, I was in six battles—Lexington, Independence,
Blues, Westport, Mines Creek, and Marshall. . . ." The old gentleman's
voice trailed off. Doubtless young Kathryn spent many an hour at her
Grandfather Walkenhorst's knee, listening to him recount those Civil
War days. He was known to be an articulate gentleman who, in later
years, was affectionately called *the Colonel* by the townspeople. It is not
difficult to imagine Kathryn saying, "Tell me more, Grandpa."[8]

"The war was tragic—a Civil War is the most dreadful of all wars.
It was a tragic confrontation from start to finish—four years of bloody
encounters. It began as a struggle to save the Union, but in the end it
became a crusade to free the slaves. I remember going with my father
to Lexington as a boy and overhearing some wealthy landowners discussing the probability of war over the slavery issue. I remember them
referring to the Germans in Concordia as 'the Dutch' and not being able
to understand our sympathies for the slaves.

"Lafayette County had her full share of misery during the Civil War.
Missouri was a border state, and each contending army fought hard for
it. The Union side wanted to keep Missouri from seceding and the
Confederate side wanted to get her to join the Confederacy. Our little
village of Concordia suffered. There were four attacks on our community
in the course of the war and some twenty-six people were killed.

"The institution of slavery had existed for hundreds of years, and was not only considered legitimate, but some thought that slavery was divine from what the Bible tells about Ham.

"But a great change in regard to slavery was soon to take place. Apparently Providence had planned to beat out slavery from our great country, and the time He had chosen to carry out His plan was when I was just a young man. . . ."

Grandpa Walkenhorst knew his history because he lived through it. "Of the thirty-two states at that time, fifteen were slave states. Missouri was one of them. A feeling of uneasiness existed in the minds of the slave owners."

Can the reader imagine young Kathryn's interest in what her grandfather was relating? "There were many rich slave owners living between Davis Creek and the Missouri River. They owned large farms and from half a dozen to twenty or more slaves—men, women, and children."

The dignified-looking Colonel came out of the Civil War unscathed, but the memories were there. The Germans, about whom he spoke, were some of the first settlers arriving in Lafayette County, Missouri, as early as 1839, among them the Kuhlman clan in 1853.

Kathryn's paternal grandmother, Catharine Marie Borgstedt, was born in Kirchspiel, Werthe, Kreis Halle, Westphalia (Germany). She married Henry Kuhlman in 1852 and one year later they embarked on the voyage for the United States to become farmers in Concordia, Missouri. The town itself was not to receive its name until 1865. It was a good name that was chosen—one befitting its residents—the name meant *harmony.*

Quite possibly Kathryn's grandparents bought their land directly from the government at the going rate in those days of $1.25 (or less) an acre. Taxes on such acreage (140 acres) was a grand total of $4.85 in 1853.

The German immigrant of the mid-nineteenth century was extremely proud of his background. And well he might be. It took tremendous self-discipline and endlessly long, hard hours of work to tame the wild prairie into well-drained farm lands. Their resources were the soil, the timber, the water, and the strength of their own bodies and minds.

These early settlers were indeed hardy people. This was virgin land, untouched by man. If they were going to farm it, they had to tackle the tough prairie sod with man-high grass. Then there was the added problem of drainage. Kathryn's father was one of nine children who had to help the family get ahead as they worked together to wrest a living from this tough prairie land.

Timber was plentiful along the many creek bottoms and so their houses were made of logs. HELP EACH OTHER OR PERISH could very easily have been their motto. Neighbor helping neighbor in the way of early pioneers. Crude plows pulled by oxen made their way slowly through the fields with the men and boys following along behind. The women spun yarn and wove cloth from the sheep they raised in order to provide clothing for the family members. Such was the life of the ancestors of Kathryn Kuhlman, herself a hearty woman whose endurance is a matter of record. Perhaps we can all understand that endurance better now— she came by it quite naturally.

Not only were these people industrious, but they had a firm reliance in God's help. They kept their faith as they faced a dangerous and uncertain future. The Walkenhorsts were Methodists; the Kuhlmans were Baptists.

Kathryn's maternal Grandfather Walkenhorst kept what he called "a memory book." In it he recorded his memories and impressions of those early days. In 1870 he was married to Hannah Kuester; they had six children.

In 1874 when the first public school was built in the community, William F. Walkenhorst was hired to teach fifty pupils at fifty dollars per month. He was thirty years old, and had a two-year-old daughter. Her name was Emma. When Emma was nineteen years old she married Joseph Adolph Kuhlman.

William F. (the Colonel) Walkenhorst was a respected citizen of the small village of Concordia. Later, he was to become the community's postmaster. But the blood-drenched struggle foisted on the nation in the Civil War left its mark on Concordia and her citizenry. Kathryn Kuhlman's wanderings as a child took her over the very streets where brave men had fallen—victims of guerrilla bands. Her grandfather and others remembered only too well.

Young's History of the area and the era relates that the Civil War was noted for these lawless bands of men, known as bushwhackers and guerrillas. They did not enter either army, but kept up a constant annoyance by their semiorganized efforts and general sympathy and aid to the Confederacy. Among these bands were men without patriotism or character, who devastated the country, killing innocent people. Bushwhackers were known to burn houses, and in some cases to tie the occupants of the houses in their beds and burn them up with their houses. The accounts are numerous of the atrocities the people endured. In misery, terror, and death, it was felt that the people of Concordia, Missouri, suffered as much as any other community in the state.[9]

When we walked the streets of Concordia in March 1976, there was not a single black man, woman, or child living in the town. But it was not always that way. In 1860, Lafayette County (of which Concordia was a part) contained a greater number of slaves than any other in the state. One-third of the county were black and slaves.

It was into this environment that Henry Kuhlman came with his wife in 1853. Eight years later they found themselves situated at the crossroads of the marching armies of both sides.

Kathryn's father was born in 1866. The war was over. The blue-clad Union armies and the gray-clad forces of the Confederacy were no more. It was rightly called "the irrepressible conflict." But now progress was to come to Concordia. At the time of Joe Kuhlman's birth, Concordia boasted of a half-dozen houses, a few vacant store buildings, a mill, a blacksmith shop, a tailor shop, a saddle shop and a hemphouse. There was no grocery store! It took three days to make the trip to Lexington, some twenty-five miles away, by ox team and wagon, where the villagers went for groceries and supplies.

In the post-Civil War period things began to happen. Miss Martha Johannssen, who was to hand Kathryn Kuhlman a hanky in the Methodist Church (the day Kathryn came into her first encounter with the Presence of the Holy Spirit), remembered those recovery days very well and wrote about it in her memory book. She wrote:

> Every Saturday the stagecoach would come through here and bring the mail. After that they surveyed and built the Lexington Branch

railroad. . . . After the train was running, we got our post office and a
drugstore. . . . There were some churches around here in the country
—the Lutheran north, the Evangelical east, the Baptist south, and the
Methodist west about two and a half miles.

The railroad actually came to Concordia in May of 1871. One year
later, Kathryn's mother, Emma Walkenhorst, was born. Early photos, in
a collection kept by the local newspaper publisher, show the interest the
people had in the steam locomotive. But train time was noted by everyone in the community. It meant different things to different people.

Fifty years later the train still meant something to the people, and in
particular to a tall, red-haired girl with a generous sprinkling of freckles
across her nose and face. One of Kathryn Kuhlman's best friends during
her school days, recalled with pleasure the fun times she and Kathryn
shared. "During those school years and until she left Concordia, we and
several other girls were good friends and chums and saw a lot of each
other. As you can imagine, in that little town over fifty years ago there
was not much going on, so we relied on our own resourcefulness for
entertainment. But we really didn't feel deprived as young people today
might feel.

"We walked on the railroad tracks to the next town four miles away,
timing our arrival there so that we could ride home in glorious style on
the humble Missouri-Pacific branch line." In his reminiscing, Kathryn's
Grandfather Walkenhorst often referred to the coming of the railroad
as being the thing that made the town spring up as if by magic.

"Regardless of all adverse circumstances," Kathryn's grandfather
wrote in his memory book, "Concordia has been building up gradually.
. . . It wears the aspect of a beautiful and healthy town; the future
prospects are better than they ever have been, and in a few years
Concordia will stand among the first inland towns of the west. . . ."

The year in which William F. Walkenhorst was writing this was 1876.
Little did he realize that 100 years later his own granddaughter would
place Concordia on the map to be recognized internationally! One
wonders what William Walkenhorst would have thought about that!

4
Without Honor

*. . . "A prophet is honored everywhere except in his own
country, and among his own people!"*

Matthew 13:57

"TURN THAT RECORDER thing off!"

We were sitting in the Concordia, Missouri, home of a woman about
Kathryn Kuhlman's age on March 13, 1976. It was the first spoken
indication I had as to the nature of the woman's reaction to the purpose
of our visit. First impressions can be wrong, but, sadly, my immediate
first impression was to be proven correct.

"You were a friend of Kathryn Kuhlman's in childhood, I understand." I smiled what I hoped was a pleasant smile at her.

"Oh, I wouldn't necessarily say that," she snapped back.

"But you did know her as a child and as a young girl?"

"Well, in a small town like this, everybody knows everybody."

(Indeed! I had already learned that!)

Our visit was short. The lady was not a Kathryn Kuhlman admirer.
She didn't want to talk about her recollections of her childhood friend.
Oh, there were innuendos and snide insinuations, but nothing based on
fact.

"Had you ever gone to one of her meetings?" I suspected what the
answer would be even before she looked at me with disdain, not saying
a word.

"Then you didn't go to any of her meetings?" I waited, giving her an
opportunity to correct me in case I'd misinterpreted her look. When no
reply was forthcoming I continued my line of questioning. "What did
you think of her books?"

"Her books? Why should I have read her books?"

I wanted to say, "Why? Why not! After all, she was from your own town, she grew up with you, you attended the same school. She was used mightily by the Lord." But I didn't voice my feelings, instead I calmly replied, "Then you haven't read her books?" Again I waited. There was no answer.

Shortly thereafter we left. I felt that I should shake the dust off my feet. No wonder Jesus said to His disciples when He sent them out as apostles and gave them instructions, "and when ye come into an house, salute it. And if the house be worthy, let your peace come upon it: but if it be not worthy, let your peace return to you. And whosoever shall not receive you, nor hear your words, when ye depart out of that house or city, shake off the dust of your feet."[10]

This same kind of reception was to be found elsewhere in the small village of Concordia, Missouri, but none was quite so cool as this woman.

In each instance where I encountered a certain coldness, my line of questioning was similar. And in each case Kathryn Kuhlman's books had not been read, nor had the individuals ever attended one of her meetings. Neither had they had anything to do with her for over fifty years. Their attitudes were based upon girlhood memories, but one sensed they had been fed from each other's storehouse of largely imagined incidents.

The encounters did not shake our confidence in the fact that Kathryn Kuhlman was chosen of the Lord for a worldwide ministry whose dimensions may never be known in the here and now. I could, however, as a result of this experience, more readily understand why Miss Kuhlman had said with such a faraway look in her eyes and a pained expression in her voice, "Someday I want a book written. . . ."

I was beginning to fathom just a little bit more the extent of the things Kathryn Kuhlman left unsaid through the years. What we experience in our childhood and growing-up years *does* leave its mark.

The day we visited her in the Shrine Auditorium she said, "My ministry is so different now." I sensed then that she was looking back through the years. That day she suddenly came back to the present, smiled and continued, "You see, I have grown so in the Lord. The greater the battle in life, the greater the boldness the Lord gives. In everything He gives what we need for the given time," and there were tears glistening in her eyes.

To myself I thought: *Battles? What does the world's best-known woman preacher know about battles? Hasn't she always known popularity and success, adulation, and prosperity?* "In order for someone to empathize with others with such compassion, they've usually been through the fire themselves," I commented to her. "Have you known personal tragedy and heartache?"

"What you said is *so* right, *so* true," she replied, bending over toward me, hands clasped tightly together. Then she straightened up, put her head back, closed her eyes, and paused before replying with deep concentration. "I want a book written . . . yes, someday I want a book written . . . I never talk about my own personal life, you know. But you are so right, you cannot feel for someone else in their sorrow, for instance, with that depth of feeling unless you've had it too."

Joe and Emma Kuhlman allowed Kathryn to leave Concordia following her sophomore year of high school. Their oldest daughter, Myrtle, had married a traveling evangelist and moved, it is believed, to the West Coast.

In a letter written from Seattle, Washington, and dated in 1924, Kathryn wrote one of her best friends in Concordia and said, "Oh, _____, tell me all about the happenings in Concordia 'cause I'm always anxious to know all the affairs, and they interest me so.

"Must close and get ready for dinner. Be sure you write at once and tell me all the news."

She signed the letter, "Your ole tormenter and tease, Katie." In the letter she shared some of the mischievous escapades in which she had a part at the boarding school she was attending. Kathryn wrote her several long letters after she left Concordia. This friend, and others in Concordia, believe she actually did attend a school somewhere, possibly out West. "She wrote telling of her pranks and high jinks there, like climbing out the window with her roommate at night to roam around a little when the rules ordered them to remain in their room and study. By today's standards these escapades were probably very mild; also she might have embellished them just a little to impress a friend left behind in the little hometown!"

Kathryn had come into a deeply moving religious experience. Did the young Kathryn see the situation in her hometown for what it was, and that it would not offer an opportunity for her to become what she wanted to be, and did she ask to leave to prepare herself for the work of an evangelist?

Edna (Pape) Sargent, now a resident of Leawood, Missouri, but a former Concordia resident and another childhood chum of Kathryn's, felt that Kathryn's sister, Myrtle, had a great deal to do with helping to train Kathryn to be an evangelist.

While in Concordia we stopped at the little Methodist church where the first major turning point of young Kathryn's life took place. It was an unpretentious little country church, small, with two aisles, three sections. Kathryn visited it in May 1972 and signed the guest register. Later she was to remark that it hadn't changed much at all, "There were the same pews, pulpit, and I think the same piano."

Roland Petering, a Concordia neighbor who was to become a well-known Kansas City banker and attorney, remembers the revival services held at the little Methodist church. "They were very emotional experiences," he states.

In her writing and in her speaking, Kathryn Kuhlman often told of her experience of salvation. "Little did I know," she said, "that my introduction to the Holy Spirit was also at the time of my conversion.

"But my experience of salvation was so definite that I have never doubted it for one second! It was at the close of a Sunday morning service in the little Methodist church in Concordia, Missouri."

Can the reader envision the scene? The eager young face upturned listening to the minister. "I was standing beside Mama, and the hands of the church clock were pointing to five minutes before twelve o'clock noon. I can't remember the minister's name or even one word of his sermon, but something happened to me. It's as real to me right now as it was then—the most real thing that ever happened to me." The way she said it, and the look on her face, you knew she was reliving the moment.

"As I stood there, I began shaking to the extent that I could no longer hold the hymnal, so I laid it on the pew.

"I continued to tremble; this was my first experience with the power of God. I sat down in the pew and sobbed. I was feeling the weight of condemnation and I realized that I was a sinner. I felt like the meanest, lowest person in the whole world. Yet I was only a fourteen-year-old girl.

"Altar calls were never given in that little Methodist church. I had often seen them take in new church members, but this was much different for me! I did the only thing that I knew to do: I slipped out from where I was standing and walked to the front pew and sat down in the corner of the pew and wept. Oh, how I wept!

"A dear little old lady, Martha Johannssen, a cripple who was considered 'too religious' because she had actually voiced her convictions regarding a literal hell, slipped to my side and I remember her whispering so tenderly, 'Don't cry, Kathryn. You've always been such a good girl.' Then she very gently slipped her handkerchief into my hand."

Kathryn would pause when telling that and say in an aside, "We both knew that wasn't quite the truth—I was one of the most mischievous kids in town!"

At the outset the tears were those of a penitent; then the recognition came over young Kathryn's being that this was an occasion for joy. "I remember turning to Martha Johannssen and explaining that now I was crying because I had just become the happiest person in the whole world. The heavy weight had lifted. I experienced something that has never left me. I had been born again, and the Holy Spirit had done the very thing that Jesus said He would do: . . . 'he will reprove the world of sin, and of righteousness, and of judgment' (John 16:8). In that moment the blood of Jesus Christ, God's Son, cleansed me from all sin.

"As we walked home from church that Sunday morning after the service everything looked brighter, more beautiful. I was sure Mr. Kroencke had gotten a new paint job on his house. But the house hadn't changed! Concordia hadn't changed! Kathryn Kuhlman *had* changed! I wonder now if my feet even touched the ground! My heart was as light as a feather and I knew why—Jesus had come into my heart. There was no doubt in my mind after that. I knew that I knew that I knew. That was surely the beginning of everything.

"My poppa never overworked this thing of going to church, and I'm putting it mildly. Oh, sure, Christmas when I gave a recitation, or on special occasions, but it had to be very special. But that Sunday I walked into the house and said, 'Poppa, something's happened to me. Jesus has come into my heart.' Whether he understood or not, I'm not sure. I never knew. He just looked at me and said, 'Kathryn, I'm glad.' But it was surely the beginning of something that changed my whole life. That experience is as real to me today as in the very hour that it happened!"

The Apostle Paul told young Timothy that in the last days it was going to be very difficult to be a Christian. They will have a form of godliness, Paul said, but will deny the power thereof. "From such turn away."

As we turned away from the house in Concordia, whose occupant was not friendly to the memory of Kathryn Kuhlman, I looked up at my husband and said, "It happened to Jesus too!"

When Kathryn returned to her hometown, Concordia, Missouri, in Lafayette County, Missouri, and taught there via television, she astonished everyone with her wisdom and the miracles.

"How is this possible?" the people exclaimed.

"She's just Joe Kuhlman's daughter, the drayman's child, and we knew Emma her mother and her brother Earl. And her sisters, Myrtle and Geneva—they lived here. How can she be so great?" And they became angry with her!

Then Jesus told them, "A prophetess is honored everywhere except in her own country, and among her own people!"

And God could do no great miracles there through Kathryn Kuhlman, because of some of the people's unbelief.

Matthew 13:53–58, paraphrased by the author

5
Kathryn the Young Girl

And whatsoever ye do, do it heartily, as to the Lord, and not
unto men; Knowing that of the Lord ye shall receive the
reward of the inheritance: for ye serve the Lord Christ.
                                        Colossians 3:23, 24 KJV

WHILE THERE WERE those in Kathryn Kuhlman's hometown who did
not appreciate her and the worldwide ministry that was uniquely hers,
there were others with an open mind and a warm heart who welcomed
us and our inquiries.

Alfred Schlapper, our genial host, "the town patriarch," as Roland
Petering (Kathryn's neighbor and childhood friend) called him, remembered the village when it boasted of a population of 800. The 1976
population figure indicated 2,100 inhabitants.

The countryside has not changed too much in the last hundred years.
The county is still settled by people with German ancestry, the land is
still highly cultivated, the heavily wooded creek bottoms still exist as do
the running streams and rolling prairies. Today there are vast fields of
golden wheat and diversified crops. There are dairies and cattle raising.
Industry has moved into the area bringing with it employment opportunities for the people.

As we drove through the lovely little village we were impressed with
its cleanliness, the well-kept homes with their gardens and orchards in
back. Roland Petering remembered the beautiful flowers which en-
hanced the attractiveness of the Kuhlman property at 1018 Saint Louis
Street. "Whenever I saw Kathryn's television program and the profusion
of beautiful flowers on the sets, I was reminded of her mother's flower
garden. When I saw Kathryn in 1972 at a Kansas City miracle service,
I reminded her of this."

The homes were mostly two-story frame buildings in Kathryn's day;

35

they still stand, some with grape arbors covering the walkways between house and summer kitchen. The Kuhlman home was large—two stories and set on a wide expanse of yard—neat and well kept.

Some confusion must have existed in Kathryn's mind about her birthplace. Rudi Plaut, chairman of the committee working to erect a permanent marker in honor of Kathryn Kuhlman on Main Street, showed me a letter from her in which she specifically stated that she was born in the family home in town. She wanted the record set straight since the local committee and others through the years had said she was born on the Kuhlman farm southeast of town.

Alfred Schlapper set about to straighten out the record. It was William H. Petering and his wife, Meta, who sold Joe Kuhlman the land on which he had the family home built on Saint Louis Street which, at that time, was the main street of Concordia. This transaction took place on February 23, 1909, according to the document in the Recorder's Office, Lafayette County, Missouri. Mr. Kuhlman bought the large piece of land for the grand total of $650! The Petering family lived next door to the Kuhlmans, and it was their son, Roland, who spoke with such kindness of the Kuhlman family, and Kathryn in particular. Kathryn was born two years prior to this, on May 9, 1907, at the Kuhlman farm, according to the record extracted from the old family Bible (which belonged to Kathryn's father's parents, the John Henry Kuhlmans).

Dora Flandermeyer, a lifelong Concordia resident, remembers going to the Kuhlman farm home with her mother to visit Emma Kuhlman and her new baby daughter named Kathryn.

"Kathryn and I didn't share the same birth date," says Fern (Kroencke) Cullom, another childhood friend, "but we were both born in the springtime of 1907, and often talked about it."

When Joe Kuhlman moved his family to town he went into the dray business. The automobile age, however, was upon them, and soon the draying business would have its demise.

William Petering and Joe Kuhlman, neighbors, were, in Roland Petering's words, ". . . lifelong friends. It was a sad day for my father, as well as the Kuhlman family, when Joe Kuhlman died. Our mothers were good friends too," he says. "Kathryn's Grandfather Walkenhorst was a well-educated gentleman. Kathryn was very fond of him, and he of her. He was one of Concordia's most eminent school professors. I have read things that he wrote, and he used flawless grammar; his English was just beautiful."

Telephone service came to Concordia in the beginning of the twentieth century. Kathryn grew up knowing what it was to call "Central," the operator of the switchboard, which was located in the Central Drug Store.

In the winter of 1908–1909 some homes and stores were wired for lights in the village. People were known to complain when their bill ran over $1.50 per month and they called the Runge Bros. (who brought electricity to the town) "daylight robbers."

Such was the situation in the community where Kathryn Kuhlman was to spend the first fifteen years of her life.

Alfred Schlapper's wife, Ella, taught Kathryn in the fifth and sixth grades, and Alfred recalls his wife's often talking about "that dramatic Kuhlman girl."

"If I'd known she was going to become famous, I'd have spent more time watching her," the Concordia residents said in one way or another. Nevertheless, she left her mark primarily because she had such a dramatic flair.

"Kathryn's mother was proud of Kathryn and this speaking ability," Roland Petering recalls. "She frequently did readings for Ladies' Aid meetings. This contributed, I'm sure, to her expertise in later years as a dynamic speaker. Kathryn led our Epworth League young people's meetings many times, and always with much meaning."

Confirmation of Kathryn's natural ability to speak with such expressiveness and meaning came from numerous sources. Everyone, it seemed, remembered this quality about her. "I was really sad when Kathryn told me she would not be returning to our high school for her junior and senior years, but was going to attend a boarding school where she would receive evangelistic training. I knew I was losing a fun-filled friend who was a kind of catalyst to the rest of us; sometimes she was too daring and even a little kooky, but she was someone whom I loved as a good friend."

This same informant spoke with strong feelings about other facets of Kathryn's character. "[For entertainment] we would hike into the country, crossing green pastures and fields which seldom carried a NO TRES-PASSING sign. It was on one of those hikes that Kathryn crawled over a barbed wire fence in her short skirt (jeans and Levis were unheard of) and suffered a deep long scratch in her upper thigh which quickly put an end to that hike. Several days later at school recess time she raised her skirt to show me how angry and livid the wound still looked. I was horrified and asked her what her mother had said when she saw it. I was surprised to learn that she had not told her mother or anyone else about the serious injury and wasn't going to. I mention this as one little example of Kathryn's independence and self-reliance and desire to do things her way."

This was a dominant trait in Kathryn Kuhlman that was to increase through the years; but it was a forceful drive that God used.

This same friend provided additional insights into the girl Kathryn. "With her large features, red hair, and freckles, it could not be said of Kathryn that she was pretty. She wasn't dainty or appealingly feminine in any sense of the word. She was taller than the rest of 'our gang,' gangly and boyish in build, and her long strides kept the rest of us puffing to keep up with her.

"Her manner was rather brash instead of ladylike, and I daresay she often tried the patience of her mother who was apt to be more rigid and inflexible in her views. Perhaps there were clashes between them (a conjecture on my part), and that is why in later years Kathryn publicly spoke very seldom about her mother except to say that she was devoutly religious, which indeed she was.

"In her books and on her TV programs Kathryn frequently mentioned her father who, in his easygoing way, was probably more indulgent toward her than was her mother. But I liked Mrs. Kuhlman and really knew her quite well because, although my family were members of another Protestant church, I was permitted to go to the Methodist church on Sunday afternoons and attended the small class which Mrs. Kuhlman taught (The King's Heralds). Kathryn would be there, of course, and a few other girls, and although all of us had already spent an hour or two in our churches in the morning, we didn't mind sitting through another hour of religious instruction under Mrs. Kuhlman.

"Later on when we were in high school, sometimes I would go with Kathryn to Sunday-evening services at the Baptist church which is where her father was a member, although he did not attend regularly."

Kathryn Kuhlman herself was very open about her father's "peculiarities" when it came to preachers. "There are those who wonder about my background and my family," she would say. "Many take it for granted that my father was a minister and that I came from a very 'religious' family. The truth is my father had an aversion to preachers. . . ."

Kathryn's high-school chum revealed the mischievous nature of her friend: "It was at one of the Baptist church evening services that Kathryn was particularly mischievous. Instead of joining in the singing of the congregation, she would flip through the pages of the hymnal and, quick as a flash, she would whisper in my ear about the titles, but not as they were printed. She would transpose words to give them a humorous twist. I would giggle, but we also both felt a little guilty afterwards because we realized we were misbehaving. The rapidity with which she did this made me think that she had engaged in this same game before. Although half a century has passed, I still remember Kathryn's mischievous streak. . . ."

Kathryn and her friend were very typical girls obviously. No wonder Kathryn recognized this same streak in teenagers and enjoyed it. Confirmation of this came (*prior* to receiving this word from Kathryn's school friend) from Dave Wilkerson who related that the first time Kathryn saw his youngest daughter, Bonnie, ". . . she laid hands on her and said, 'This girl is more like me than anybody I've ever met.'

"I said to her, 'Kathryn, how do you know that?'

"She said to me, 'Dave, I bet I could read her off to the letter . . . she is mischievous. . . .' and I said, 'She sure is!'

" 'Yes, she has a mischievous streak in her . . . Dave, this girl is going to have a ministry. . . .'

"And do you know," Dave Wilkerson said to us, "most of the things Kathryn prophesied about Bonnie are true."

The point here is, however, that Kathryn recognized a mischievous streak in Bonnie Wilkerson because she herself had, at one time, been a mischievous fun-loving young girl.

In her school work Kathryn was an average student. There were those who said they felt her flamboyant nature was not conducive to sitting still long enough to study in depth as some subjects required. "Kathryn's strength lay in any school activity where her flair for dramatics and organization could be put to good use, and that's where she really shone," said her close friend of those days.

"At school parties she was always put in charge of games and entertainment, and it could have been here that she had her first public-speaking lesson. I remember so well an incident when she was trying to get our attention to teach us a game. She was having no success whatsoever trying vainly to rise above our din with her own high-pitched voice (at that time) and rapid-fire delivery, until our teacher said, 'Kathryn, if you lower your voice, and speak more slowly they'll listen to you.' And so we did!"

What an amazing revelation this was to me! I trust the reader sees the far-reaching effects of this and the long-lasting impression it made on Kathryn Kuhlman. Kathryn's mother had often told her to slow down also, and work to "speak distinctly." Those of us who criticized her for the way she spoke, with such deliberateness, and in such a dramatic way, should now realize (once and for all) that there *were* reasons for this and they already had their origin when Kathryn was a very young girl.

"Kathryn was an extrovert of the first water and an organizer with a real talent for leadership. One time in high school she decided that things were getting a little dull, so she organized some of us girls (about six or seven) into a club and talked a store owner into letting us use an empty upstairs room for our early evening meetings. Our activities were completely innocent and the name she gave us was J.J.'s, and as I recall, the letters meant Jazzy Janes. Or was it Jolly Janes?"

Kathryn's activities in subsequent years were lost to this friend. As happens so frequently, we lose touch with those with whom we shared many growing-up experiences. However, when Kathryn Kuhlman was thrust into prominence because of the miracle services and her books, TV programs and radio broadcasts, once again her Concordia girl friend began following her activities with renewed interest.

In a letter dated July 31, 1972, to Harry R. Voigt, historian and professor at St. Paul's College in Concordia, Kathryn wrote:

> Standing by the side of House Speaker Carl Albert and Senator Jennings Randolph, all three of us having been conferred with Honorary Degrees, was a very outstanding moment of my life; but believe me when I tell you to have the people in my hometown honor me with their suggested idea was a much greater thrill!
>
> It is not because it means so much to me personally, as much as the fact it also represents my poppa—Joe Kuhlman—for the people of Concordia would not have the same respect for me today that they have, were it not for the example of my father and mother who lived all their lives in Concordia.
>
> This letter gives you my permission to have the proposed sign placed on the highway stating that Concordia is the birthplace of Kathryn Kuhlman. . . .
>
> With our faces toward the sunrise, let us be faithful to our Master with that which He has given us—ever mindful of the fact that our ability is always the measure of responsibility. He shall judge us, not by the obscurity or the prominence of our service, but by the faithfulness with which we performed it . . . .

The marker to which she alluded was to be placed in close proximity to the well-known Concordia historical marker commemorating those brave people whose lives were taken in the Civil War conflict. History will now not only record that Concordia, Missouri, was the site for this memorable though tragic incident, but future generations and those presently living will be able to say, "This was the birthplace of Kathryn Kuhlman; she was a member of the Baptist church, an ordained minister of the Evangelical Church Alliance, known for her belief in the Holy Spirit."

In another letter to Gary Beissenherz, editor of the local paper *The Concordian,* Kathryn Kuhlman wrote:

Be assured that I feel greatly honored to have the people of "my hometown" honor me be erecting an historical marker noting Concordia as my birthplace!

I have always been proud of the fact that I was born in Concordia where the people are still "the best in the world" and they continue to remain the very salt of the earth with sound principles and morals that have not changed with the changing times. My early training did much to influence my life. . . .

As Rudi Plaut (Concordia businessman) said: "Anyone of that stature deserves recognition. People who grew up with her cannot comprehend the magnitude of her recognition worldwide and her influence."

6

"I Just Carry a Water Bucket for the Lord"

". . . if, as my representatives, you give even a cup of cold water to a little child, you will surely be rewarded."
Matthew 10:42

SHE'S BEEN CALLED by many names. Labeled and titled, some complimentary, others not so kind. *Time* magazine said, "She is, in fact, a veritable one-woman shrine of Lourdes."[11] The *Los Angeles Times* called her "the red-haired phenomenon."[12] Others have said she is the "Queen of the Faith Healers," "The Miracle Woman," "Kathryn Kuhlman, Superstar," and other titles.

By whatever name that was attached to her and the ministry that was uniquely hers, Kathryn Kuhlman said of herself that "I just carry a water bucket for the Lord." This was a consistent emphasis throughout our conversation.

But the record stands up under scrutiny. What other Christian woman has made such an impact around the world with such astounding results? What other Christian woman had her books translated into fourteen different languages; or sold over three million copies of just one book?

The day I walked about the farm where Kathryn Kuhlman was born, I saw two old-fashioned red pumps, one by the house, another out by some of the farmyard buildings. It was not at all difficult to imagine Kathryn's mother priming the pump to bring up water for her family. I could visualize her struggling with a full water bucket. This woman, who was to have such an influence on the lives of her daughters, in particular, also carried a water bucket for the Lord in her own way.

"Mrs. Kuhlman was really, I'm quite sure, the spiritual leader of the home," said one gentleman whom I talked to who knew the family well. "Kathryn's mother influenced my own life greatly, as did Kathryn even when we were in grade school."

Roland Petering was very fond of the flaming-red-haired, vivacious young Kathryn. "I remember so well how she pulled me along Sunday after Sunday to what was called 'The King's Heralds' meetings over at the Methodist church. Mrs. Kuhlman was the teacher, and she was good. I can remember her to this day and those meetings. . . ."

Fern (Kroencke) Cullom has clear recollections of those Sunday-afternoon meetings also. "We wouldn't have missed that for anything. She was an excellent Bible teacher and Kathryn and her sisters and brother must have received very fine teaching and training at home."

Even though Kathryn was three years older than Roland Petering, she always included him in their Sunday-evening young people's meetings as they got into their early teens. "I wasn't a Methodist, but I sure enjoyed going to Epworth League with Kathryn. Fern went to those meetings also. The Kuhlman family was very musically inclined," Roland Petering recalls. "We were neighbors and on summer evenings we could hear someone singing and someone else playing the piano. That was pleasant," he says in recollection.

Other childhood friends remarked about Kathryn's musical talents.

Young Kathryn dearly loved her father. "I loved my poppa more than anything else in the world," she said on many occasions. She was proud of the fact that he served two terms as Concordia's mayor. Petering, in describing Mr. Kuhlman said, "He always reminded me of Abraham Lincoln because he was tall, slender, and a rather quiet type of gentleman."

Joe Kuhlman had a son Earl whom townspeople remembered as being quite different from his famous sister, Kathryn. "He was older than Kathryn," Roland Petering explained, "and everyone knew him as Kooley. Earl was mechanically inclined and I was always fascinated by the various types of racing cars which he built near the big apple tree where Kathryn and I shared so many happy hours.

"It should be kept in mind that in that era racing was done primarily on dirt tracks at county fairs, Fourth of July celebrations and, of course, the Missouri State Fairs at Sedalia, as well as surrounding states. After building several racers according to his own specifications, Earl finally acquired a super type of racing car which was alleged to be the fastest vehicle on wheels in those days. Racing cars at that time required two people, the driver and a [mechanic] companion seated next to the driver who was needed to pump oil inasmuch as the engines did not have adequate lubrication systems. As I recall the stories circulating in those days, Earl found it difficult to get anyone to accompany him in his new fast racer, and his elderly father, I understand, expressed no fear and rode with him during several races."

One can't help but wonder if Kathryn stood on the sidelines cheering them on, at the same time nervously worrying about the safety of her beloved poppa and big brother!

Other Concordia residents also remember Earl's genius for mechanics. "He had a flying service," says Alfred Schlapper. "He'd land in the pastures; those were the days of the barnstormers. Earl was one of them! Out east of here he had painted on a big barn: EARL KUHLMAN'S FLYING SERVICE."

Kathryn's brother also left behind a reputation.

"He knew how to spend old Joe's money," said one man. "If Kathryn was famous as a 'woman preacher,' Earl was talked about locally but in a different way."

Woman preacher. Kathryn would have laughed in a good-natured way at that. Maybe there were those who called her that in her hometown, but elsewhere around the world she maintained that no one really thought of her as a preacher. At a meeting in which she discussed the Baptism of the Holy Spirit, she commented: "You ministers, uhhh . . . remember, I'm really not a preacher, not really. Not really . . . that's the reason when you say you don't believe in women preachers, I don't either. When you think about it, I don't think that anyone ever considers me as a preacher. When you think of Kathryn Kuhlman, I don't believe anyone thinks of me as a woman preacher—not really. I don't think of myself as a woman preacher—*never!* Nobody refers to me as Reverend Kuhlman. Oh, that's the funniest thing. You never think of me in that light, do y'? Never! And I don't think of myself in that light, believe me, because I can't preach.

"All that I know is that I'm somebody who loves the Lord with all my heart. I just love the Lord . . . He's so wonderful. So if you've come here today to hear me preach a sermon, forget all about homiletecs . . . I don't even know what it means. I'm just hear talking to you about the Lord and my own personal experiences. . . ."

What did Kathryn think of Kathryn?

When asked on a San Francisco TV talk show what she called herself (a frequently asked question)—faith healer? evangelist? minister?—she quickly replied: "I am not a faith healer. I resent being called that more than anything. I am just an ordinary person. I really don't know what I am other than just somebody who loves people and wants to try to help everybody that I can. I'm not a faith healer because I've never healed anyone. It's just the mercy of God." Not a preacher. Not a faith healer.

What would Kathryn Kuhlman have entitled her autobiography? Quite possibly exactly what she called herself: "I'm just a water-bucket carrier."

Notwithstanding the fact that she did not consider herself a preacher, she did stand firmly on the fact that her call to the ministry was as definite as her conversion. "If everybody in the world told me that as a woman I have no right to preach the Gospel, it would have no effect upon me whatsoever, because my call to the ministry was as definite as my conversion."

When *Christianity Today* magazine asked her: "How have you overcome the disreputable cloud in which faith healers operate?" she unhesitatingly answered.

> I have not overcome anything because I do not put myself in a class with faith healers. It's only the news media that have put me in that class. As I said before, I am not a faith healer. I have not been given anything special. What I have is something that any Christian could have if he would pay the price of full surrender and yieldedness. I am absolutely dependent on the mercy of the Lord Jesus Christ. I am dependent on the power of the Holy Spirit in exactly the same way that Jesus was when he was here in the flesh and walked this earth. . . . A faith healer? No, I merely remind you how big God really is.[13]
>
> (Copyright 1973 by *Christianity Today*, used by permission.)

Kathryn liked to refer to herself as "a handmaiden of the Lord." There are several biblical references to that terminology. (*See* Luke 1:38, 46–48.) In the Old Testament, Joel, the prophet of Judah, spoke a prophecy that was picked up by Peter in the Book of Acts. There, in Acts 2, Peter, filled with the Holy Spirit, stood up on the day of Pentecost and preached that great sermon in which he quoted the prophecy:

> And it shall come to pass in the last days, saith God, I will pour out of my Spirit upon all flesh: and your sons and your daughters shall prophesy, and your young men shall see visions, and your old men shall dream dreams: And on my servants and on my handmaidens I will pour out in those days of my Spirit; and they shall prophesy.[14]

Did Kathryn Kuhlman see her ministry as a return to the supernatural element in the early Church?

"Everything that happened in the early Church, we have a right to expect today," she answered my question. "My own role is only that of an intermediary; one of many upon whom the manifestation of the Holy Spirit's power has been poured out.

"Oh! You want to know something? This is the Church's greatest hour. I'm expecting to see the manifestation of the power of the Holy Spirit in the next years as we have never seen it before. Remember, time is running out, *the time of the end is running out,*" she repeated it, her long finger pointing.

"I believe in the rapture of the Church, and that we will be caught up before all of the tribulation, all of the suffering. But oh, the power of the Holy Spirit . . . everything, absolutely everything that happened in the early Church is going to happen again before the catching up. I'm talking about miracles such as we have never, never seen before.

"I believe that is the reason the enemy of our souls is fighting the way he is against miracles, against the manifestation of the power of God. And so, we just hold steady . The enemy knows. The enemy knows what the future holds really for the manifestations of God's power. So all we can do is hold steady. There will be miracles that will astound the world. "

7

The Idaho Years

*But God has chosen the world's foolish things to put to
shame the learned. . . .*

1 Corinthians 1:27 MLB

WHEN KATHRYN KUHLMAN was six years old she gave a surprise birthday
party for her mother. She invited thirty of her mother's friends and
asked *each* guest to bring a cake. Doing surprising things on a grand
scale was to be the pattern of Kathryn's life. But it wasn't always that
way.

When Kathryn left Concordia, prior to her junior year in high school,
it was with the definite feeling (in her words) "that I wanted to serve
the Lord . . . but I didn't know how."

The first thing she did was to answer an advertisement for a cook to
work on a nearby Indian reservation. "I couldn't cook so much as an egg!
But I did think I wanted to go help the Indians.

"They never even answered my letter. I suppose they didn't want a
fourteen-year-old. But I was heartbroken. You see, I always wanted to
do nice things for people—to make them happy—."15

She started out in the ministry as a teenager defending Christ and the
Bible. "After years of experience," she said, "I found out that He needs
no defense. He will defend Himself. As for the Holy Spirit, all I have
to do is to be faithful to preaching the Word, and He will defend me."

Her spiritual education really began, however, in Idaho. "I think so
very often these days everybody wants to start at the top rung of the
ladder. Everybody wants to be a big preacher, a great preacher, a famous
preacher, a wealthy man, a celebrity . . . I know where I began. I know
from whence I have come."

She told of sitting at her kitchen table one Sunday morning at five
o'clock thinking back to those times. "I was to preach in Youngstown,

48

Ohio, that morning, but I'd gotten off the plane at midnight. I was weary in body and had gotten very little rest; I found myself weeping, all alone in the house. The tears were falling on my open Bible and I just looked up and said audibly to my Heavenly Father, 'Oh, dear Jesus, why didn't You allow all this to happen to me when I was sixteen years of age?' You see, I never got tired of body then . . . I didn't know what weariness of the body really was . . . I could ride those buses all night and then preach all day. All I can remember is that I didn't need sleep at all. 'Why did You wait so long, wonderful Jesus?'

"There wasn't an audible voice . . . I would tell you an untruth if I told you that I heard an audible voice . . . but He did speak to me as definitely as though I could see His Person and hear His voice: 'Kathryn, had I given it to you then, you would have blown the whole thing!' And I knew exactly what He meant!"

One of the most outstanding qualities of Kathryn Kuhlman (almost without exception everyone would agree) was her great sense of humor. She could laugh at herself; she could make fun of herself, point out her own weaknesses and what she considered glaring deficiencies—and laugh. And in the process she had everyone else laughing. On or off the platform she was marvelously funny.

"There was a growing process," she stated. "There was a time of learning, a time of schooling—oh, not in some seminary nor some university—the greatest Teacher in the whole world is the Holy Spirit. Believe me, you'll get your theology straight when the Holy Spirit is your Teacher. I studied my Bible, oh, how hungry I was for the Word of God!"

She was hungry in other ways too! She remembered very well those days of never seeming to need much sleep, but also of always being "so hungry. Sometimes there was only the price of a bowl of soup. Rolls were five cents (my, that was a long time ago!). It seemed I was hungry all the time."

In those early days of her ministry she needed every cent she could scrape together for posters and handbills which she had printed to advertise her meetings. Pictures taken in those days show that the freckle-faced, red-haired little girl had developed into a tall, slim beauty.

An old-time preacher used to say that when they'd put up posters to announce her coming to a town to preach the people would flock to her meetings because they could expect to see "sex and salvation." She was a typical woman and brushed that aside with an embarrassed turn of her head when I mentioned it to her.

"Those days I never stayed at a hotel. I never even thought of staying at a hotel, and I don't think they had many motels then. But sometimes a deacon and his wife would put me in their guest room. (Those dear Idaho farmers were so kind to take me in.) But I would lie on my stomach in bed and just pour over the Word of God, studying and reading.

"Oh, I know who has been my Teacher! I know why I know what I know today regarding the Word of God. It didn't just happen, my friend," she would say. "Nothing ever 'just happens,' and you never get something for nothing even when it comes to spiritual things—always remember that.

"I remember overhearing someone say once, 'My, but she's a lucky girl.' They were referring to my ministry even then when I was still in my teens. But it wasn't luck! I know the price that I paid—I know the price. So all I could preach was salvation."

And preach it she did!

At first she had to almost beg to be allowed to preach, but that soon changed when word got around about "the young girl evangelist."

Many little churches across the Midwest had been closed. Many towns were too small to support a church and a full-time minister. "They had nothing to lose," she would modestly say, "so they let me preach."

When I made contact with people around the Caldwell, Idaho, area, I found many families who still remember those days. "Her ministry had a real impact on the entire Valley where we lived," stated Freada Planting of Boise, Idaho. "Kathryn was a very dynamic speaker even then. Some even criticized her already at that time for being too dramatic. I remember it all so well. But it didn't stop the people from filling the churches to capacity. Back in those days the denominational fences were pretty distinct, but it didn't keep the people from coming from *all* denominations. We had her in our Baptist church, and people who

had never 'darkened' the door of a Baptist church before would come!
"And her altar calls! Yes, she surely did have old-fashioned altar calls.
Kathryn insisted on a real born-again experience."

Freada's maiden name was Fretwell.

"My father, William Fretwell, backed her meetings wholeheartedly,
and most of them were held in the small Baptist churches scattered
about throughout that whole Boise Valley.

"Her deep spirituality and the way she conducted her services is, I
am sure, the reason my father sensed that she was Spirit-filled already
then. He asked her if she was and she told him, 'Oh, yes!'

"My father helped support her those years during and after she left
the Valley. Many times she wrote asking for prayer when the going was
rough. While we lived in Roswell she spent much time in our home
because she truly felt she had the spiritual backing there.

"Papa's support was not very large as there were twelve of us children,
and he believed in supporting his own church with his tithe, but he was
such a generous man when it came to the Lord's work, and always gave
over and above his tithe. When my sister, Frances, saw Kathryn in San
Diego a few years ago, they were talking about Papa and Kathryn said,
'That man! That man! He never knew *all* he meant to me!' She said
that *many* times she was down to her last dime or her last pair of
stockings and my father would slip some money into her hands if she
was here, or it would come in the mail from him just when she needed
it the most."

What was Kathryn Kuhlman like in those days out of the pulpit?

"She was always very relaxed and just a very normal person. And yes,
so much fun to be with. She dressed like any of the rest of us. We would
get together and sit on the grass or the church steps and just visit. She
enjoyed going on picnics and we did have some good times! Kathryn was
such an average person, *so* nice, *everybody* loved her, and she loved us
in turn; we could all feel it. But in the pulpit, Kathryn was *all* business
for the Lord.

"I remember talking to her one day about feeling a call of the Lord on my own heart and she told me how she started out herself. 'The call of the Lord just seemed to consume me,' is what she told me. She also told us how her parents thought she was much too young to leave home; however, she just couldn't give it up. She actually went to a neighboring town and stayed in a chicken coop that some lady cleaned out for her. She told me about spending five cents on a butterhorn roll. That's really how she got started.

"Kathryn was a very modest person. She dressed very plainly in the pulpit. She had a seamstress make her several dresses—pink, blue, and yellow, out of a soft crepe material. They were made exactly alike with box-pleated skirt, full, long sleeves cuffed at the wrist. She didn't want to draw attention to herself even in those days. Both she and Helen Guilford, her pianist, dressed modestly in the style of the time.

"Helen, too, was a quiet person and yet her presence and love of the Lord was so deep. They were a great team.

"Kathryn's meetings were from two to four and sometimes six weeks in length. People would drive for miles to attend them, even in the busy summer months and those were farming communities. Our family attended all her meetings within a ten to twenty mile radius, and that was a long way to go in those days—especially after the men would put in a hard day in the fields. Papa would just quit work early enough to get the chores done (milking and feeding) and get us to the meetings. Then he'd be up at four-thirty the next morning for another long day in the fields.

"But we kids were always anxious enough to go to the services that Papa didn't have to prod us to get our work done. I was sixteen or seventeen at the time. Kathryn must have been in her early twenties on this second time in our area.

"Kathryn was just as dramatic with her hands and facial expressions and voice then as she had been in later years. This, plus the fact that she was a woman, brought much criticism from many people—but amazingly, she still filled the churches and had many, many converts. She really was loved by young and old alike. Women preachers, outside of the Pentecostal churches, just weren't too well accepted in those days, but it didn't hinder her meetings. And her ministry at that time was mostly in the little community Baptist churches."

Freada Planting talked to other Idaho people who recalled the Kathryn Kuhlman meetings held in the Emmett Valley in the small towns of Ola and Sweet "up in the hills out of Emmett. She held meetings in Nampa in an old store building, but to my knowledge all her other meetings were held in the small community Baptist churches in Notus, Wilder, Caldwell, Melba, Meridian and Kuna (in addition to Roswell where we lived)," Freada commented. "There may have been others as well." When Kathryn Kuhlman told curious reporters how her ministry all began and stated, "Name any little town in the State of Idaho, and I worked at trying to evangelize it," she was putting it mildly!

She would say to those interviewing her: "The very first sermon I preached was about Zaccheus up a tree, and God knows that if anyone was up a tree I certainly was! I remember the sixth sermon I preached —I honestly felt I had exhausted the Bible." But, according to Freada Planting, Kathryn was being modest.

Freada corresponded with Kathryn's sister, Geneva, until 1936 or 1937. "We corresponded with Kathryn and Helen about that long too. They sent us their papers and literature from Denver. Then, after that, we lost contact with her until 1945 when my husband and I were visiting my uncle in Portland, Oregon. She was holding meetings there. This was where she originally had met Helen Guilford.

"From then until she came into the miracle ministry on radio and then television we had no more contact. . . ."

Kathryn said of those years: "If I had to go back to those little churches tomorrow, if I had to speak to only a handful of people, I'd work just as hard. I loved those people. I would gladly have given my life for them, my flesh and bone."

Of Kathryn's move to Denver, and later her marriage, Freada Planting said: "We really never knew much of anything about her marriage. I just know she couldn't divide her life between a husband and her work for her lovely Jesus. The Lord was her very life—all her life."

Mrs. Marie Sleeper from Caldwell, Idaho, remembers Kathryn's staying at the home of her parents, Mr. and Mrs. Oliver P. Pennington, in Notus, Idaho.

And a Mr. Emil Koble of Caldwell, Idaho, who was a farmer and a stock man, took Kathryn and Helen to different churches in the Caldwell area and has good memories of those days.

John and Ellen Sasenbery of Nampa, Idaho, attended the meetings. "The time that the girls were in the Melba, Nampa, area was the year of 1924 in the fall, and in the spring and summer of 1925. Miss Kuhlman was about the same age as my wife (sixteen years old) at that particular time," Mr. Sasenbery states.

"Oh, those little country churches in Idaho!" Kathryn Kuhlman said. "I'm still getting letters from some of those precious farmers . . . and members of their families who say, 'We remember you well. . . . we see you now on television. But we remember you as the young girl who came to our church. We remember you as the one who preached so simply . . . you haven't changed, y' know . . . !'

"That's the greatest compliment that anyone can pay me. To say to me, 'It's still the same; you haven't changed.' Why should I change? The Gospel is the same! The Word of God is the same and I pray to God I will never change.

"I used to wait until those farmers were through with their milking, their plowing, their harvesting, and when it got dark they would file in one by one. I've been in every one of those little crossroads towns— everyone. If the town didn't have a preacher I offered my services. Nobody really wanted me—I didn't blame them much—but I did say to them, 'Your church is closed anyway. You haven't anything to lose, and you might gain something.' "

Yes, Kathryn Kuhlman—they did gain something! They gained something that they have never forgotten or lost. *You left them a great legacy.*

8
The Silent Years

. . . and the Spirit of Jehovah came upon him and gave him
great power from that day onward. . . .

1 Samuel 16:13

"SOMETIMES I THINK the reason I have such a depth of feeling for people is that I can forgive so easy. Y' know, I've been forgiven so much, so that it's easy for me to forgive others. Maybe that's the reason I see the tenderness of the Lord and that's the reason I know of His great compassion. It's more than theology with me. And so when anyone really knows my background and what I've been through, then they understand me better. But I don't talk about it."

We were discussing at this particular point the subject of divorce. "Oh, yes, it's so easy to sympathize; it's so easy to understand when you've been through it. But to those who have never been through it, it's so easy to criticize. It's the easiest thing in the world to criticize.

"But I just feel sorry for them, people who criticize . . . yes, I just feel very, very sorry. . . . But oh, I could never tell you the protection I have . . . *The Lord is so faithful. . . .*"

The implication was plain—others may prove unfaithful, others may hurt us in the worst possible way—but God is ever faithful.

It was at this point that she repeated again that perhaps someday she would write a book and reveal more. Since her death, a number of news reports have come out with comments about her marriage and divorce.

. . . . For almost 20 years she led congregations around the Midwest. By the time she was in her early twenties, she was pastor of a 2,000-seat red-brick church in Denver.

There she met a traveling evangelist, Burroughs Waltrip, who di-

vorced his wife to marry Miss Kuhlman in 1938. The union did not last
and Miss Kuhlman, repenting, closed that chapter of her life, never to
remarry.[16]

I have talked to several people who were members of Kathryn Kuhlman's Denver congregation. Vonetta Hardy with her husband, Dillard,
and three children regularly attended Kathryn's services and remembers
those days very well. "Kathryn came to Denver with five dollars. She was
preaching on Larimer Street in a little mission. I happened to hear her
over the radio; I liked her voice (very southern), and went down. I think
the year was about 1934. She had a pianist with her, Helen Guilford,
who has since passed away."

Of those Denver years, Kathryn herself was quite silent. "Her radio
broadcast was called 'Smiling Through,'" Vonetta Hardy recalls. "It
wasn't long until she was invited to come up to our Denver Revival
Tabernacle at Ninth and Acoma."

When I questioned Mrs. Hardy about Kathryn's personal life, the
possibility of a marriage and a divorce occuring during those years, she
said, "I don't know anything about that," and the subject ended.

Another former Denver resident who was a tiny girl when Kathryn
pastored the church which her parents attended, was Mrs. Paul Ferrin.
(Paul Ferrin took Dr. Metcalfe's place after his death as choir director
for Kathryn's services.) "My parents, James and Thelma Daniels, still
live in Denver," Mrs. Ferrin said. "My father once told Kathryn Kuhlman that he had never seen such compassion in a person. He told her
then that as long as she maintained this compassion and love for people
there would be no end to what God would do in her life."

Mrs. Ferrin sang in Kathryn's services in Denver as a small child. "My
parents felt that those five years or so which she spent in Denver were
probably some of the happiest years of her life. She had great love for
other people's children and would often take me by the hand, get my
parents' permission, and take me places.

"My father says that no matter who was at the altar at the end of a
service, Kathryn stayed with them until their needs were met. She truly
showed great compassion."

When I asked Mrs. Ferrin if she or her parents wanted to say anything about the heartache that came into Kathryn's life, her reply was a quick, "No, we never discuss that."

I had to admire the loyalty of these people. Much speculation has been set forth regarding Miss Kuhlman's personal life; some of which I have read and heard.

I spent a number of hours with Russell Chandler, Religion in the News editor of the *Los Angeles Times,* and we discussed, among other things, Miss Kuhlman's reported marriage and divorce and the silence surrounding it. Writers and reporters with a Christian background have, for the most part, respected Miss Kuhlman's wish for privacy and have not belabored the issue regarding this part of her life. Mr. Chandler and I were in agreement that we, too, should respect that wish for silence on Kathryn Kuhlman's part. Mr. Chandler reported with restraint:

> The little-known facts about her marriage and subsequent divorce dealt a severe blow to her burgeoning Denver Revival Tabernacle. Evangelist Burroughs A. Waltrip, who had been a guest speaker in Miss Kuhlman's pulpit, liked more than her church. Divorcing his wife, Waltrip married Miss Kuhlman in Mason City, Iowa, on October 19, 1938. The marriage soon dissolved, however, and in the heat of the scandal, the Denver congregation scattered. Miss Kuhlman, who never remarried, was loathe to discuss the matter. Oldtimers are quoted as saying she suffered over it and repented.[17]

"I had a sorrow, I had a heartbreak," she has admitted about that period of time in her life.

But miracles started personally for her following the most unusual religious experience of her life, and it is generally believed this came about at the time of this deep personal tragedy. She spoke of walking down a dead-end street and realizing that her life was a dead-end street. "It was four o'clock on a Saturday afternoon. It was at that time and in that place that I surrendered myself fully to the Holy Spirit." She often said that there are some things too sacred to talk about, but in that moment, with tears streaming down her face, God and she made each other promises. ". . . He knows that I'll be true to Him and I know that I'll be true to Him. In that moment, I yielded to God in body, soul, and spirit. I gave Him everything.

"Then I knew what the Scripture meant about taking up your cross. A cross is the symbol of death. That afternoon, Kathryn Kuhlman died. And when I died, God came in, the Holy Spirit came in. There, for the first time, I realized what it meant to have power."[18]

The stigma that accompanies divorce is of the cruelest kind. Today it is not nearly as severe as it was at one time—the time particularly when Kathryn Kuhlman went through it.

"You knew she was divorced, didn't you?" I was asked by a number of Concordia, Missouri, townspeople. The way it was said, you could feel the revulsion. Divorce is undesirable, but I find nothing in God's Word that says it is unforgivable! My heart aches as I think of what Kathryn Kuhlman must have endured in trying to rise above the criticism. In no way can she be faulted for being protective about her past and wishing for silence. She suffered much and worked hard to overcome this and rise above it. God saw the anguish in her heart. He reads motives. He knew all that had happened—the behind-the-scenes problems that victims of divorce cannot possibly reveal. Kathryn knew she could safely entrust herself into the Father's hands and that in time He would vindicate her. And God did just that.

And so, Kathryn left Denver.

God has divine vision. Who else can make that claim! Kathryn recognized that. It gave her new hope—that and the experience of the indwelling Holy Spirit. God's standards of right haven't changed through the years; but neither has His vision!

In talking to Allen Spraggett, Kathryn said: "When I'm in that miracle service I'm a different person. Would you believe me if I told you that at such times I don't even associate the name Kathryn Kuhlman with myself. That's true . . . when the Holy Spirit is upon me I'm a different person. . . ."[19]

She repeatedly emphasized that "in a real sense, Kathryn Kuhlman is dead." She was always deeply emotional when making that statement.

Her life was complex, and the change about which she spoke was so profound that an actual reference to the first part of her life was like talking about someone who was dead.

David Wilkerson observed that "her marriage and divorce almost cost her her ministry, her very life. I think she made up her mind that from that point on no man was going to get near her. (In a way she may have been taking it out, in a sense, on men ever since in some of her working relations with them. This would be understandable.) I have heard all kinds of stories, but I cannot find it in my heart to judge her for her past any more than David the psalmist was judged. I think it's what a person is at a particular time in their life, and at the time I worked with her she was a great woman of God. I didn't really care about her past. I wouldn't have cared if she'd been a harlot—God had done a great work in her life. You see, it didn't matter to Jesus!"

9

Kathryn Confronted With Death

Keep me as the apple of the eye, hide me under the shadow
of thy wings.

Psalms 17:8 KJV

(Portions of this chapter are taken from an article entitled "My First Healing" in GUIDEPOSTS magazine and are reprinted by permission from GUIDEPOSTS magazine, Copyright © 1971 by Guideposts Magazines Associates, Inc., Carmel, New York 10512.)

"I HAD THE MOST perfect father a girl ever had. In my eyes Poppa could do no wrong. He was my ideal.

"He never spanked me. He never had to. All he had to do was get a certain look on his face. Mama wouldn't hesitate to punish me when I needed it. But Poppa punished by letting me know I had hurt him—and that hurt worse than any of my mother's spankings.

"When I was a little girl I used to have terrible earaches. Mama would pour sweet oil in my ear and use all the home remedies she knew. But the thing that eased the pain best was for Poppa to stay home from work, take me on his lap in the rocking chair, and let me lay my aching ear on his shoulder."

With that kind of love for her father, returned by him to her, known and experienced in such a special way, it was no wonder that news concerning him affected her deeply. This bad news came while she was in Denver. She was renting a room in the St. Francis Hotel (Room 416 for four dollars a week) from a Mrs. Holmquist. "It was there at 4:30 P.M. on the Tuesday after Christmas in 1934 that the phone rang. I recognized the voice on the other end as an old friend from home. 'Kathryn, your father has been hurt. He's been in an accident.'

" 'Hurt—bad?'

" 'Yes,' she said.

" 'Tell Poppa I'm leaving right now. I'm coming home.'

"I had bought an old V-8 Ford and I threw a few things into the back and started out. Only God knows how fast I drove on those icy roads, but all I could think about was my father. Poppa was waiting for me. Poppa knew I was coming."

Those who have lived in that part of the country, or experienced such weather conditions, will fully appreciate the driving hazard she faced. "The weather got worse as I drove out of Colorado into Kansas. The roads were covered with ice and drifting snow, but I didn't stop to eat or rest."

One hundred miles from Kansas City, which is about sixty-five miles west of Concordia, she stopped at a telephone station beside the deserted highway and called ahead. "My Aunt Belle answered," she related.

"I said, 'This is Kathryn. Tell Poppa I'm almost home.'

" 'But, Kathryn,' Aunt Belle said in a shocked voice, 'didn't they tell you?'

" 'Tell me what?' I said, feeling my heart begin to pound madly in my chest.

" 'Your father was killed. He was hit by a car driven by a college student who was home for the holidays. He died almost instantly.' "

Kathryn was stunned. When she tried to speak no words came out. "My teeth were chattering wildly and my hands shaking as I stood in that forlorn phone booth, surrounded by the swirling snow. I can only remember the biting wind freezing the tears on my cheeks as I stumbled back to my old car and resumed my trip homeward."

The miles between Kansas City and Concordia were a nightmare to Kathryn. She was twenty-seven years old and had not faced the specter of death so close to home in such a traumatic way before. Even though she had been away from home for some eleven years, the memories she carried with her of her father were very dear ones. Travel in those days was very expensive for a young woman, particularly in that kind of work. She needed every penny she could get for handbills, newspaper space, and storefront rental in addition to expenses for mere survival. Her times home in those years had been few and far between. Now she was going home to be confronted with death—the death of the one person in all of Concordia who meant the most to her.

"The next miles were like a nightmare. The highway was a glare of ice. Mine was the only car on the road. Night fell and my headlights shone back at me from a wall of blinding white. I was crying, trying to hold the car on the glassy road."

To herself she thought: "I've got to get there . . . Maybe it isn't true. Poppa can't be dead. It's just a bad dream . . . Maybe it will go away."

But it didn't go away, and when the physically exhausted daughter of Joe Kuhlman arrived home, one of the saddest experiences of her life awaited her. The big frame house on Saint Louis Street rose up out of the gloom of the darkness to greet her. "My father's body was in an open casket in the front room." This was the custom of the day. She was lovingly greeted by other members of her family, but her heart was torn with grief—her poppa was not able to take her in his long strong arms and hold her close. She fled to the refuge of her bedroom upstairs.

"I could hear the soft shuffle of feet on the front porch and the whispered talk around the house." She didn't want to go down and face the reality of her father's death. It was like a bad dream.

Kathryn's friend Fern Cullom remembers the incident very well. "It was a bitter blow; they were so fond of each other. My uncle was the coroner and doctor of Concordia. Uncle 'Doc' said that Mr. Kuhlman was deaf and had a habit of walking with his collar up, especially when it was cold weather. My uncle said, however, that he was not convinced that the car actually struck Mr. Kuhlman.

"When I went to see Kathryn and her mother at the home, Kathryn was grief-stricken. It was a shock to see her that way, and it was a shock to her family as well, and to the whole town for that matter."

Kathryn herself admitted to struggling with feelings of hate. "It surged in me like a volcano and to everyone who came into the room I spewed out venom . . . I had always been a happy person, and Poppa had helped to make me happy. Now he was gone and in his place I was battling unfamiliar strangers of fear and hate."

The day we spent in Concordia, Missouri, some forty-two years later, we sat in Topsy's Cafe, the local eatery, which existed back in Kathryn's day under the same name. The cafe was owned by the Oetting family. "It was the Oetting boy who was driving the car that (supposedly) struck and killed Joe Kuhlman," Alfred Schlapper related as we sat sipping our coffee.

"How did it happen, Al," I asked. "Do you remember the incident?"

"Yes," he replied, "Mr. Kuhlman went to get two dozen eggs. He was carrying them home in a paper sack. The streets were covered with ice and he fell. Of course the eggs broke, so he went back to get some more and it was then that the car came along. Joe was jaywalking across Main and Ninth streets. I can still see him, he was a familiar figure because he always walked with his collar up around his ears. Joe was deaf. . . ."

The story was pieced together from two different sources, each related it to me separately, but the accounts were the same.

Kathryn related how God helped her to work through her grief and, in so doing, enabled her from that time on to minister in an even more personal way to those who experience heartache and grief.

"Then came the day of the funeral. Sitting there in the front row of the little Baptist church, I still refused to accept my father's death. It couldn't be. My poppa, so full of love for his 'baby,' so tender and gentle, it couldn't be that he was gone.

"After the sermon, the townspeople left their pews and solemnly walked down the aisle to gaze one last time into the casket. Then they were gone. The church was empty except for the family and attendants.

"One by one my family rose from their seats and filed by the coffin. Mama. My two sisters. My brother. Only I was left in the pew.

"The funeral director walked over and said, 'Kathryn, would you like to see your father before I close the casket?'

"Suddenly I was standing at the front of the church, looking down —my eyes fixed not on Poppa's face, but on his shoulder, that shoulder on which I had so often leaned. I remembered the last conversation we had had. We were in the back yard . . . he was standing beside the clothesline, reaching up with his hand on the wire. 'Baby,' he said, 'when you were a little girl, remember how you used to snuggle your head on my shoulder and say, "Poppa, give me a nickel"?'

"I nodded, 'And you always did.'

" 'Because it was what you asked for. But, baby, you could have asked for my last dollar and I would have given you that too.'

"I reached over and gently put my hand on that shoulder in the casket. And as I did, something happened. All that my fingers caressed was a suit of clothes. Not just the black wool coat, but everything that box contained was simply something discarded, loved once, laid aside now. Poppa wasn't there."

Kathryn had been preaching for some time, but in her words, "This was the first time the power of the risen, resurrected Christ really came through to me. Suddenly I was no longer afraid of death; and as my fear disappeared, so did my hate. It was my first real healing experience.

"Poppa wasn't dead. He was alive. There was no longer any need to fear or hate.

"Numerous times I've been back to the little cemetery in Concordia where they buried the body of my father. There are no tears. There is no grief. There is no heartache, for that morning in church I knew the Apostle Paul's words to be true: 'To be absent from the body is to be present with the Lord' [*see* 2 Corinthians 5:8].

"That was many years ago. Since then I have been able to stand at the open grave with countless others and share the hope that lives in me. There have been mountaintops across those years, opportunities for travel and ministry and preaching. But, you know, growth has come not on the mountaintops but in the valleys.

"This was the first valley—the deepest—the one that meant most. When I walk offstage today, after hours of confronting sickness and deformity and need in every form, I go back to the dressing room. And often at that moment I have a strange feeling. I feel that Poppa is there. He never heard me preach, in earthly form, but I know he knows that his girl is trying to do a good job for the Lord. And he knows that now I constantly lay my head on the shoulder of the Heavenly Father, knowing I can claim all the blessings of heaven through Jesus Christ."

We saw the cemetery in Concordia where Kathryn's parents have been laid to rest. The gravestone reads: JOSEPH ADOLPH KUHLMAN, APRIL 11, 1866—DEC. 30, 1934.

In 1958 Kathryn came back to Concordia to lay her mother's body alongside that of her father. The headstone reads: EMMA WALKENHORST KUHLMAN, AUG. 28, 1872—APRIL 17, 1958. There are also two small graves on the family plot where Kathryn's brother's children were laid (they died in infancy).

When we were there in March 1976, the Christmas wreath sent by Kathryn at Christmastime 1975, was still on the burial plot. "Kathryn always remembered them on special occasions with flowers and wreaths. She loved her parents very much and was always good to them," Alfred Schlapper said as we stood at the graveside. "Joe would have been proud of 'his little girl.' "

To myself I thought: *Mr. Kuhlman, what happy memories you left for Kathryn. The world owes you a debt they can never repay—you and Mrs. Kuhlman gave to the world a very special child who, in God's providence, was destined to become one of the "apples of His eye."*

Kathryn always said, "I was the apple of my poppa's eye. Just so, we are very special to our Heavenly Father—we are the apples of His eye and He wants the very best for us."

10

"I Have No Healing Virtue . . .
It's All the Power of God"

*This is my work, and I can do it only because Christ's mighty
energy is at work within me.*

Colossians 1:29

"IF YOU HAD WARTS and wanted them removed, Kathryn's mother
would take your hand and say, 'Now look at me,' and she'd just rub your
hand, tip her head back and look up. . . ." It was Kathryn's cousin (by
marriage), Ralph Erdwin, speaking. "Three or so days later the warts
would be gone!"

Whether Kathryn was aware of this, I do not know. I could find no
reference to this in any of her books or in any interviews. "Buddy"
Samuels (Ralph's granddaughter and the local Concordia librarian) was
so helpful to me. She supplied the family genealogy from the family
Bible and other information and confirmed what her grandfather had
to say.

In the early days of her ministry Kathryn was greatly disturbed over
many things that she observed in the field of divine healing. "I hated
traditional tent healing services," she explained. "Those long healing
lines, the filling out of cards . . . It was an insult to your intelligence.
Once, after visiting such a service, I cried all night. I determined that
with the Holy Spirit's help, my ministry would not be that way." Because she was confused by "methods" she saw used, and disgusted with
"performances" she witnessed, she delved even harder into the Word
of God for answers.

The sight of pathetically sick people dragging their weakened bodies
to such services and then being told that they were not healed because
of a lack of faith, made her heart ache. Man's superfluity of zeal crushed
her. She could not see the hand of God in the services she attended as

a visitor. "I think that no one has ever wanted Truth more avidly than I—nor sought it harder."

With the looks of despair and disappointment on the faces of those who were so defeated as they left so-called Divine Healing services etched into her thinking, she sobbed out her heart to God as she prayed for light on the Truth.

> Fortunately I had learned a valuable spiritual lesson early in my ministry —one which was to come to my aid now: I had learned that the only way to get the truth is to come in sincerity and absolute honesty of heart and mind, and let the Lord Himself give one the blessed revelations of His Word, and *through* the Word, make His Presence real and His Truth known.
>
> At no time in my search did I profess to wear the robe of infallibility. I did not seek as a dogmatist, nor as one with a closed mind, but only as one who was daily learning, willing to be guided by the Holy Spirit, and longing to be taught of the Father—as one who was hungry for deeper spiritual knowledge, not from man but from *God.*
>
> I waited expectantly for the answer, and it came.[20]

When Kathryn left Denver she had headed for Pennsylvania. "Think what a place God chose!" she said. It was the old Billy Sunday Tabernacle where years before the famed evangelist had stood preaching with such power.

At her first service thirty-eight people put in an appearance. At the next service nearly two hundred came. After that, the tabernacle was never able to hold the crowds. "It was in that third service, as I was preaching on the Holy Spirit—the little bit I knew about the Holy Spirit then—just before I began speaking, a woman stood up and I was shocked when she said, 'Pardon me, Miss Kuhlman, please . . . may I give a word of testimony regarding something that happened last evening while you were preaching? While you were preaching on the Holy Ghost, telling us that in Him lay the Resurrection power, I felt the Power of God flow through my body. I knew instantly and definitely that I had been healed. So sure was I of this, that I went to the doctor today and he confirmed that I was healed.' The tumor was gone!

"Without the laying on of hands, without any prayer—just a woman sitting in the audience in Franklin, Pennsylvania—while I was preaching on the power of the Holy Spirit." Every time Kathryn Kuhlman told it, she was as deeply moved as she was at the time the woman related it. "The secret?" she asked, "The Third Person of the Trinity! *The Holy Spirit, then,* was the answer . . . it's so profound, yet so simple. . . ."

The services continued in Franklin. The second miracle was the case of George Orr who received sight in his blind eye after twenty-two years. "I knew that I had tapped some great Resource . . . oh, the thrill, the joy, the expectancy!" she exulted as she gave God all the glory. "I preached again on the mighty Power of the Third Person of the Trinity and word of the miracles spread."

It was in 1947 that she decided to move her base of operations to Pittsburgh. Dan Thrapp, writing in the *Los Angeles Times*[21] said she descended on the city with the Word and her vivacity. But there was something else—no, *Someone* else—it was a special anointing of the Holy Ghost which characterized her ministry from that time forth. "That was the beginning of this healing ministry which God has given to me," she explained in her book *I Believe in Miracles:*

[The ministry has been] strange to some because of the fact that hundreds have been healed just sitting quietly in the audience, without any demonstration whatsoever, and even without admonition. This is because the Presence of the Holy Spirit has been in such abundance that by His Presence alone, sick bodies are healed, even as people wait on the outside of the building for the doors to open.

Many have been the times when I have felt like taking the shoes from off my feet, knowing that the ground on which I stood was Holy Ground. Many are the times when the Power of the Holy Ghost is so present in my own body that I have to struggle to remain on my feet. Many are the times when His Very Presence healed sick bodies before my eyes; my mind is so surrendered to the Spirit, that I know the exact body being healed: the sickness, the affliction, and in some instances, the very sin in their lives. And yet I could not pretend to tell you *why* or *how!*[22]

She was aware from the outset, however, that she herself had nothing to do with it, and that it was the supernatural power of Almighty God. "If I knew the answers to the *why* and *how,* then I would be God," she said. "I am satisfied to leave it all to Him."

She rented the city-owned Carnegie Auditorium for two weeks that stretched into six months of services, and then on instructions from Pittsburgh's mayor (who was later to become the state's governor), David Lawrence, she was told she could stay in the auditorium as long as she wanted. That turned out to be twenty years. The Kathryn Kuhlman Foundation offices were established in the Carlton House Hotel and remain there to the time this is written.

When Carnegie Auditorium was renovated, the spacious First Presbyterian Church in downtown Pittsburgh, under the leadership of its pastor, Dr. Robert Lamont, invited her to hold weekly services there.

On the occasion of the anniversary of twenty-five years of service in Pittsburgh, a special celebration was held at Pittsburgh's Hilton Hotel. It was a beautiful and memorable occasion with 2,500 guests honoring this woman whom they esteemed so highly. People came from all over the country for the occasion. It was a lighthearted, fun-filled evening in which many participated.

Logos magazine reported that it was a night of remembering. Most of all, it was a time of Kathryn Kuhlman's thanking the people of Pittsburgh in particular—and America in general—for their love and confidence given over twenty-five years of ministry.

A couple who knew Kathryn when she conducted services in Franklin, Pennsylvania, are Bob and Ruth Atkins.

The Atkinses later lived in Akron, Ohio, and were faithful in attending Kathryn's services held at the Stambaugh Auditorium in the neighboring city of Youngstown. "Kathryn considered her Youngstown friends her family," Ruth Atkins shared. "She often told us to come to the services fasting and praying. No matter how much she was traveling, she always arranged to be in the Pittsburgh area at Christmastime. The Christmas programs were very special. The highlight of our daughter Nancy's life was being chosen to be the 'Littlest Angel' when she was four at one of these Christmas specials. Miss Kuhlman was dressed in a black jumper and white blouse and played the part of a Sunday-school teacher telling the story to a class of little ones. On the opposite side of the stage, the scenes were acted out. At the close, Miss Kuhlman held Nancy's hand and led the congregation in singing the old familiar Christmas carols."

When the Atkins family moved to California, they commuted to Southern California or to the Bay area every time Miss Kuhlman held services. "Her ministry was our church," they often told us when we lived in the same city (Salinas, California). "Kathryn Kuhlman more than any one person has made Jesus real to me," Ruth Atkins says. "I remember much she has said, and through the years I've drawn on her teachings constantly. She always stayed with the Word, and often told us that if she said one thing and the Bible said something different, *she was wrong,* the Bible would always be right.

"We are grateful to have had our children raised in this ministry for they learned young that if they put God first, everything else would fall into its proper place."

11
What Made Kathryn Kuhlman Tick?

For as many as are led by the Spirit of God, they are the sons of God.

Romans 8:14 KJV

" 'YOU KNOW WHAT I am in the flesh—I stink—and You know there is nothing worse than Kathryn Kuhlman in the flesh. Lord, I don't want to touch the gold, or the glory—I'd rather die. You get all the glory or I cannot go out there and minister . . . !'

"Mascara was running down her cheeks as she cried out in prayer. She thought she was hid behind the curtain, but I was close enough to hear her pray," Dave Wilkerson described his first meeting with Kathryn Kuhlman as we sat in the lovely blue-carpeted sitting room off his office at Twin Oaks Ranch, Lindale, Texas.

David Wilkerson, founder of Teen Challenge and the David Wilkerson Youth Crusades, first came into contact with Kathryn Kuhlman when his best-selling book *The Cross and the Switchblade* came to Miss Kuhlman's attention. "She invited me to conduct a crusade in Youngstown (Ohio). This was rather exciting because in my mind she was really a very strong personality.

"I respected her greatly because everyone in religious circles in the greater Pittsburgh area knew of her. Actually I'd known about her all my life, since my father pastored a church in Pittsburgh. She was controversial even back then in her early days in the Franklin area. But when I was just a young teenager I would hear her on the radio. My parents talked about how she was packing in the crowds in Pittsburgh. Long before some of the healing evangelists came to the fore, she was already well established with a very legitimate healing ministry. She had some kind of a charisma which was implanted in my mind even though I'd never been to one of her meetings. So that when *The Cross and the*

Switchblade had become popularized and when she did contact us for meetings, I was anxious to find out what made Kathryn Kuhlman tick.

"I don't remember that first meeting too well," he says, "other than that her mannerisms at first turned me off. I do remember my first impression when I saw her backstage and she greeted me—she was in a hurry. Later I was to discover that she was always in a hurry. I decided then and there that I'd find out what *really* made her tick.

"I was very curious, I must admit," he admitted in our conversation. "I watched her choir file in and they seemed to have such a reverential awe—to my mind she was kind of drinking it in. I thought to myself, *I don't know how God can bless this—it seems to me like an ego trip.* But just a few minutes later is when I saw her go behind a curtain and heard her pray. . . ."

As David Wilkerson talked that day to us the modulations in his voice underscored the feelings he was trying to convey. "To myself I said, *'Oh, boy, is this the secret? The way she appears on the outside, that's just exterior. She has an inner humility that You look at?'* And then she introduced me as a man of God," Dave paused in the telling as he relived the moment.

"This is Dave Wilkerson," Kathryn Kuhlman was saying, "I have discerned him to be a man of God." Can the reader identify with David Wilkerson in that moment?

I questioned Dave: "She followed very carefully the leading of the Holy Spirit? She was very obedient to that inner voice, wasn't she?"

"Yes," he replied without a moment's hesitation, "I was most impressed by this. At that first meeting, for instance, there was no way she knew that I was within earshot and could hear her pray before she went out. She really thought she was hidden—but I just happened to be right where I could not only see her, and she *not* see me, but also where I could very plainly hear."

I, too, had wondered what made Kathryn Kuhlman tick and had, in fact, asked her that very question outright. "Oh, it's all on the inside of me," she clasped her hands across her chest and tilted her head to the side. "You can't give to anyone else more than you have yourself. Every morning the first thing I think about when I awaken is: I wonder what's going to happen today? That's my mental attitude and that's the reason I am a very early riser—5:30 or 6:00. In any hotel where I stay, they know that my light will be on in the hotel room very early because the very minute it starts getting light I have to get up because I'm afraid I'm going to miss something.

"But inside of me, I know me better than any one else. I know my heart and I know that God knows my heart. That's the reason when I walk out on stage—you can be sure I know my heart, my relationship with the Lord, and that's the thing that matters most."

David Wilkerson asked Maggie, Kathryn's right-hand secretary and confidante, one time, "When does Kathryn pray? She's so busy all the time—you know her, Maggie, does she pray early in the morning? or late at night?"

Maggie had replied, "I've worked with Kathryn for years. Kathryn Kuhlman is praying all the time."

Dave remembers Kathryn's telling him once, " 'I take my secret closet with me—if I'm in a car that's my secret closet, or wherever I am—there's nothing in the Bible about being in a geographical place or location to pray—I've learned to commune with the Lord anytime anyplace.' This is but one of many great spiritual lessons Kathryn Kuhlman taught me. *Pray without ceasing!"*

When I questioned Kathryn Kuhlman about priorities and use of time and her busy schedule, and how she accomplished so much, she again emphasized: "This thing is a life. A reporter once said to me, 'How much time do you spend preparing for a miracle service?' The question threw me at the time because it was the very first time it had been asked. I said to him, 'You don't understand, *I stay prepared.* You don't prepare for a service, *I'm prepared twenty-four hours* out of the day.' I say to my ushers at the services, in our ushers meetings, 'Listen now, this is no time to have a prayer meeting—you come prayed up before you get here.' "

David Wilkerson began to wonder about Kathryn's amazing vitality. Her energy seemed inexhaustible. As he worked with her he found it difficult to keep up with her and he was much younger than she. "I'd preached for her one month when I was really very tired," he related. "I'd been very, very busy, but I came in and preached at Stambaugh and then went to the Syria Mosque in Pittsburgh. We had finished the evening service and she wanted to take my wife and me out to eat something. After a busy day like that she'd still be all wound up. So I said to her, 'Kathryn, I'm too tired. I've got to get back to the hotel. I'm just ready to pass out.'

"She looked at us and said to me, 'David, you must not know your Bible!'

"I looked at her and I mean that really surprised me, and I said, 'Well, now, what do you mean?'

"She said to me, 'Did you preach under the anointing tonight?'

"I replied yes, I had, and she said, 'Did you preach under the anointing this morning?'

"I told her yes again, and she said, 'Isn't the Holy Spirit supposed to be in us a quickening Spirit? The same Spirit that raised Christ from the dead if He dwell in you, He shall also quicken your mortal body by His Spirit that dwelleth in you.[23] David, isn't it reasonable to believe that if you're preaching under the anointing that He's going to be in the process of quickening you? You should be stronger when you finish than when you started.' She then went on to explain, 'That's the secret to my strength. People just don't realize that, but I am totally dependent on the Holy Spirit and when the Holy Spirit is moving through me, He gives me unction, He's in the process of quickening my physical body, so that if I exercise faith I can have it and claim it.' She told me that day that anything you see is yours—no rigmarole, no problem—the only way to receive something from God is to acknowledge the revelation. If you see it, it's yours. That day she said to me, 'Do you see it, David?' I said, 'Yes,' and she said, 'All right, right now it's yours. Let's go out and eat.'

"You know," David Wilkerson said to us years later, "since then I haven't had a tired moment after I've done preaching—and all it was, was a revelation of the Truth. Kathryn Kuhlman had principles in her life—those who are ever used by God have these principles which they've worked out for themselves as revealed to them by the Holy Spirit —and she believed so strongly, her faith was simply: *God said it, I believe it, that settles it*—and she put it to practice in her every experience.

"In the first place Kathryn did not choose her calling—none of us do —we're chosen by God. She was chosen by God for her calling. Second, the blessing of God is not accidental. There are prices to be paid. She was willing to pay the price. She had a very simple theology. I sat down and picked her mind for hours and hours around a table. She would say to me, 'I've never answered critics. I have to answer only to God.' "

To me, Kathryn Kuhlman had related almost the same words: "Please realize how detached I feel from the things that happen [in the services]. That is the reason why it never fazes me when the miracles and ministry are discredited, because it isn't me. I am completely detached," she emphasized.

Many old-time evangelists and early saints (in their writings) speak of this sense of detachment. It is not a new phenomenon.

"When people question and criticize, they are not attacking Kathryn Kuhlman, they are attacking something that is as permanent as God," she said.

"What makes Kathryn Kuhlman tick? In answer to your question, without the Holy Spirit I haven't a crutch, I haven't anything to lean on. I don't have a thing. You see, if I had been born with talent, I might have been able to lean on that. If I'd had an education, I might have used that as a crutch. And had I chosen a profession, in all probability my choice would have been either medicine or law. But I had no choice: I was called of God to preach the Gospel. Let me repeat: without the Holy Spirit I don't have a thing."

12
Detachment

. . . . give yourselves completely to God—every part of you
—for you are back from death and you want to be tools in
the hands of God, to be used for his good purposes.

Romans 6:13

"PLEASE REALIZE how detached I feel from the things that happen. . . ."
Kathryn Kuhlman was talking to us backstage at the Shrine Auditorium.
She explained this feeling of total detachment like this: "It's as if my
body is possessed by the Holy Spirit and as though I were removed, up
above somewhere, looking down on the proceedings. I feel as though I
am just a bystander. And to tell the truth, I am honestly just as amazed
as anyone else by the miracles. I see myself—and please believe me—
I'm shocked when I hear myself say things like: 'A cancer is being
healed.' I am just as amazed as anybody else in the auditorium at what's
happening. And I know that I have absolutely nothing to do with it. The
Bible says [Zechariah 4:6 KJV] that it is 'Not by might, nor by power,
but by my spirit, saith the Lord,' and that *is* the only explanation."

The best explanation I could find of what Kathryn Kuhlman was
trying to describe came from Dr. Don Gross, an Episcopal priest with
academic degrees in physics, theology, and psychology, including a Har-
vard doctorate in the psychology of religion. One aspect I especially
appreciated about Dr. Gross's attempts to explain this was his statement
that " . . . any descriptions I offer [are not meant] to undermine any
spiritual interpretations." He went on:

> "Kathryn Kuhlman is an extraordinarily creative woman to have
> accomplished what she has, particularly with the limitations of educa-
> tion and opportunity in her early life. What may have happened is that
> this intense person—and she has unusual intensity and energy—looking

forward to marriage and family life, in which a woman has her . . . children, is frustrated. There is a great and painful collapse of her hopes and of her wish to love and be loved. At this point she turns to God as her love object. She is going to spiritualize the energy that would have gone into marriage and family life and devote herself instead to another kind of love, love of the Heavenly Father.

"I would guess that she loved her earthly father devotedly and hoped in marriage to find the fulfillment of that first great love in her life. Out of her deep frustration of this hope she turns to the Heavenly Father who won't disappoint her.

"She is very hurt, and in looking for healing for her own heart finds that one way of being healed is to become a channel of healing to others. Sometimes the best way to make up for a disappointment in love is to give love. So, as Kathryn Kuhlman becomes a channel for spreading God's love to others, she receives that love herself and her heart is healed.

"Instead of receiving love from one person in marriage, she turns out to be the center of the adoration of many people.

"Mind you, this love from many is not fully satisfying. Like all public figures, Kathryn Kuhlman says 'I live a lonely life; I'm either with the crowd or I'm all alone.' But the difference is that Kathryn Kuhlman is not really completely alone, but alone with God. She has found such an experience of God's love and presence that it fills the void. . . . And it is this experience of God's love that makes her charismatic—the sense of God's love and presence radiates from her."[24]

When Kathryn Kuhlman said, "I know the secret of the power in this ministry, I know better than anyone else," she *really* meant it. "I know that I have nothing to do with the power of the Holy Spirit. When the power of this Holy Spirit comes upon men and women and they are 'slain' . . . I know I have nothing to do with this. When men and women are so wonderfully healed by the power of God, I know better than anyone else that I have nothing to do with it. I'm absolutely dependent upon the power of the Holy Spirit."

She liked to refer to the Old Testament saints, pointing out that the

Holy Spirit is not a new personality. "He was there at the time of creation—all three Persons were there—'And the Spirit of God moved upon the face of the waters' [Genesis 1:2]. Whenever the Bible speaks of the Spirit of God it's the Holy Spirit.

"Moses knew the power of the Holy Spirit. . . .

"And Gideon knew. . . . When you read the Old Testament and see the power that was upon those saints . . . what was it? The secret was the Holy Ghost, the sovereignty of God . . . Joseph was filled with the Holy Spirit; and Sarah recognized the power of the Holy Spirit. The Holy Spirit was no stranger to many of those Old Testament saints. Read your Bible again in the light of this, it will be most revealing.

"If we could call the Old Testament prophets together, they would bear witness to the very power of the One of whom I speak, and always it was the sovereignty of God. David knew of the Person of the Holy Spirit. That's the reason we have this cry in the Word of God of David, 'Take not Thy Holy Spirit from me.' It was the same Holy Spirit that I know. I've prayed that same prayer ten thousand times: 'Take not Thy Holy Spirit from me.'

"I'm not afraid of man or Satan. But I do have one fear lest I grieve the Holy Spirit. I die a thousand deaths before I walk out on stage. I know better than anyone else how dependent I am on the Holy Spirit," and she repeated it again. "I'm not a psychic healer. I'm human! But so often I would like nothing better than to be able to slip behind the stage curtains so people wouldn't have to look at me. I'm only a mouthpiece telling others how big God is. He is Truth and He cannot lie.

"Samson, in the Old Testament, knew not that the Holy Spirit had departed from him. Remember how he tried to get up and shake himself as other times . . . I've seen it, you've seen it, when the Holy Spirit is not there we have fanaticism and we have manifestations of the flesh, and that is what brings reproach on the Holy Spirit. You see, I love Him so much I couldn't do without Him. And this fellowship I have with Him—this communion—there are no audible words in the human vocabulary to describe it. And I almost have a sense of protectiveness toward Him. Don't bring reproach upon the Holy Spirit," she would plead. "Please, I beg of you . . . so much reproach has been brought upon the Holy Spirit. Never act contrary to the Word of God. If your actions are contrary to the Word of God, if you cannot back up your actions with the Word of God, then there's something wrong someplace with your experience. There is nothing more revolting and more disgusting than manifestations of the flesh after the Holy Spirit has departed from someone's life."

She deplored those who were "banking" on an experience of many years ago. She felt they were as "dried up as last year's corn shock."

"I too received the Baptism of the Holy Spirit many years ago, but there's never a time when I'm in a great miracle service but what I receive a fresh Baptism of the Holy Spirit. And when I stand to minister in Christ's name, I feel that anointing from the top of my head to the soles of my feet.

"You are then so under the anointing that literally your ears hear—for *He* is preaching through your mouth under this anointing of the Holy Spirit. I've stood there and He's taught me, *He's* spoken through my lips and my ears have heard and I knew it wasn't Kathryn Kuhlman."

The out-of-the-body experience and feeling which Kathryn Kuhlman spoke of has been the subject of much study by scientific and psychic researchers. But, as she herself often said, "You can't analyze it." Dr. Don Gross has stated that what she called "being caught up in the Spirit," was beautifully reminiscent of the ecstatic state reported by some medieval saints and mystics. "The root of the word ecstasy from the Greek means 'standing out of oneself.' And it is by this standing out of herself that Kathryn Kuhlman becomes the clear channel through which the healing power flows.

"However, the channel is not merely one-way. It is not merely that the power of God flows somehow through Kathryn Kuhlman and out to the people but also that the people's devotion somehow is channeled through her to God. And I think this is the key to the healings. For even though one individual in the service might not have to have much devotion to get healed, the whole group has to have the devotion to create an atmosphere in which the healings can happen. . . .

"All this is for me," said this eminent Episcopal priest and researcher, ". . . a sign and a wonder proclaiming that God is alive and loving and able to help those who seek Him."[25]

She was always thankful that she had never attempted to write a book on theology, or, in particular, on the doctrine of the Holy Spirit. "If I'd written such a book," she said, "about six months later I might have had to say, 'I've made a mistake,' because as you watch the Holy Spirit at work you discover you can't put Him in a special category, you can't put a fence around Him. He can't be fenced in! When you do, you find it isn't long before He jumps the fence and that all you've got left is a fence! No one can have a 'corner' on the Holy Spirit; He's bigger than denominational lines; He's greater than man's ideas. He's so powerful. . . ."

What she knew of the Holy Spirit came by seeing Him at work, by watching Him at work, and getting to know Him and His personality as He revealed Himself and His power to her. "I know what grieves Him; I know what pleases Him—it's like being in the presence of someone you know so well and you know when they are grieved or happy."

"Just remember," she said, "the Holy Spirit is never unseemly in His actions. If it's revolting, if it's obnoxious, it's not the Holy Spirit! Then it's flesh. . . ."

She insisted that she had never known the Holy Spirit to reveal Himself in a revolting way. "He is perfection," she insisted, "I have such high regard for Him."

She knew there were things happening today that were being attributed to the work of the Holy Spirit. "It cannot be the Holy Spirit if it is contrary to His personality, His beauty and His loveliness . . . The Holy Spirit will always magnify and glorify Jesus. There are those who run such a 'hobby' on the Holy Spirit that they have forgotten all about Jesus. Jesus Himself made it very definite that 'the Holy Spirit will magnify and glorify Me.' "

She cautioned against limiting the Holy Spirit to the 120 who were gathered together on the first Day of Pentecost (*see* Acts 2). "Without the Holy Spirit," she said in all seriousness, "I'm sunk. The longest walk I ever take is the walk from the wings [behind stage at a miracle service] to behind that pulpit. The reason I walk so fast is because I can hardly wait for the anointing of the Holy Spirit to come upon me."

Kathryn Kuhlman's birthplace on the farm southeast of Concordia, Missouri. The primitive pump, still in use, is a reminder that Kathryn often said that she "just carries the water bucket for the Lord." *Below:* The Kuhlman home in Concordia where Joe Kuhlman moved his family in 1909. The little girl on the porch may be Kathryn.

The Methodist church where Kathryn came into a vital encounter with the Holy Spirit. *Below:* The Kuhlman Family: left to right are brother Earl; Kathryn's beloved Poppa, Joe; Geneva, the older sister; Kathryn, and her mother, Emma.

Interior of the little church. Kathryn often spoke of slipping down to the front row and sitting in the corner of the pew, weeping. *Below:* The First Baptist Church of Concordia. "Poppa was a Baptist; Momma was a Methodist." Kathryn attended services in both churches.

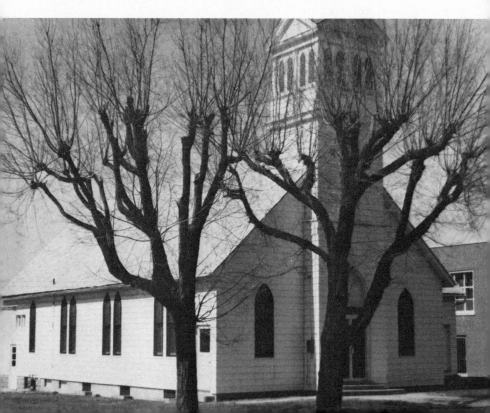

The City Hall of Concordia. Kathryn's father served two terms as mayor. The grade school attended by Kathryn. *Below:* You can find Kathryn Kuhlman in the school picture in the third row, sixth from the right. She is standing between two teachers. Her friend Fern (Kroencke) Cullom (who sent this photo) is sitting in the front row, third from the right, sporting a "spit curl."

Kathryn Kuhlman was probably about fourteen or fifteen when this picture was taken on the church back steps. Taken in the early thirties. This photograph, loaned by Mrs. Freada Planting, shows Geneva Kuhlman (Kathryn's sister), Helen Guilford (Kathryn's pianist), and Kathryn. It was taken in front of the parsonage in Roswell, Idaho. *Below:* This photograph of Kathryn and Helen was taken in Meridian, Idaho, about 1932.

In Notus, Idaho, during Kathryn's early ministry. Left to right: Oliver P. Pennington, Helen Guilford, Kathryn, and Laura Pennington. *Below:* Kathryn smiles happily at Faith Temple in Franklin, Pennsylvania, where she had such a successful ministry.

Faith Temple, Franklin, Pennsylvania
—Goes into the Hands of the People
—Through the Untiring Efforts of Kathryn Kuhlman—When the $30,000.00 Debt Was Paid Off and the Mortgage Burned on New Year's Eve

The People Sing WITH KATHRYN KUHLMAN

This is the cover of a songbook used at Kathryn's meetings during her early ministry. Kathryn at her desk, probably in the Carlton Hotel (Pittsburgh) right after she left Franklin. *Right:* In those days she had a radio ministry as well, in Western Pennsylvania.

Kathryn with Rex and Aimee Humbard at the Cathedral of Tomorrow in Akron, Ohio. *Below:* In October, 1972, Kathryn Kuhlman had an audience with Pope Paul VI who gave his personal blessing on "her admirable work." He presented her with a medallion symbol of the Holy Spirit, a dove.

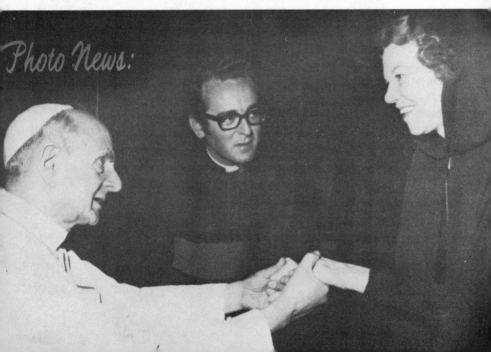

Photo News:

Those who attended her services knew what she was talking about. The state of "ecstasy" as some have described it, saw her standing very still and quiet for a few moments in what appeared to be a condition in which all consciousness of being on stage was lost. Her face was always upturned and her arms were outstretched in prayer and adoration.

She confessed that she was never quite sure what she was going to say when she walked out on a platform. "It just comes out. Later, when people tell me what I've said, I'm amazed . . . I'm completely detached. . . . To come back after the service . . . how can I describe it? It's like bringing the soul back into the body again. Believe me, it has nothing to do with spiritualism or anything like that . . . I just yield myself completely. . . ."

The Apostle Paul knew what Kathryn was talking about. It was he who admonished: ". . . yield yourselves unto God, as those that are alive from the dead, and your members as instruments of righteousness unto God" (Romans 6:13 KJV).

13
Kathryn's Frailties

I will try to walk a blameless path, but how I need your help. . . .

Psalms 101:2

"SHE'S NOT A SAINT without flaws, but she is one of My children."

Not an audible voice, but a deep inner conviction witnessing to the spirit within me. The news editor of a Christian magazine, upon hearing that I was writing about Kathryn Kuhlman, wrote to extend his best wishes and offer some well-meant advice: "There is the need for honesty, objectivity, and balance (all of us are shades of gray, with both lighter and darker hues at places)."

There were many, even those closest to her, who recognized and readily admitted that Kathryn Kuhlman had some frailties. Indeed, there were problems aplenty through the years. Many of them she caused herself; others were not so much her problems as other people's (specifically her critics).

Kathryn's admirers (of whom there were millions) will cringe at the mere mention and suggestion that she had problems (frailties). On the other hand, her critics and the fence-sitters (those who weren't quite sure which side to take) will accuse me of whitewashing the woman and failing to be objective and totally honest.

How then does one objectively and honestly reveal those problem areas? The Word of God is my authority. It has always made good sense to me to look at those whose lives have been so faithfully recorded for us in God's Word.

Time after time, as I've looked at Jesus in the Gospel accounts, I have been impressed with His love for the fallible Peter. This is a source of great encouragement, for who among us isn't like this blundering man? As I've looked at Peter and others, I've seen that their failures were as frankly dealt with as their successes. Certainly their failures were not glossed over. When I look at Peter and then at myself I take courage. And I wonder if this wasn't true for Kathryn Kuhlman also!

Kathryn was aware of some of her frailties; others she was less likely to acknowledge.

"How do you reconcile the fact that she had materialistic lusts, that she lacked a private devotional life?" her critics asked.

Allen Spraggett commented about this, observing that she was very much a woman, in her fondness for fine clothes, for instance. She took a healthy delight and a childlike pride in "the nice things" her material success had made possible. She saw no virtue in returning to the extreme poverty of her early days.

She often stated that she would rather give up every material thing than lose her sense of the Presence of God.

Regarding the accusation that she lacked a private devotional life, my response would have to be, "Did you live with her?"

Dave Wilkerson has said of her, "Kathryn had her problems, but the preaching of the cross is the most important thing and this is the reason almost anything she did was all right with me, because at the heart of it was the preaching of the cross. She preached the cross, she preached holiness, she preached divine judgment, she preached the full Gospel. Kathryn wasn't off on a lot of tangents; she would minister in the Word on her radio program; she would study hard. She was probably one of the best doctrine preachers in America. She was taught by the Holy Spirit. People think of Kathryn Kuhlman as dealing only in a healing ministry—but I think she was one of the best Bible teachers I've ever met. She had tremendous insights into the Word that were very practical. She was a practical Bible teacher. And she was respected. You talk to some of the real Bible scholars and they have respect for what she said and preached more than for her healing ministry."

It takes time and effort to prepare radio messages that go out over the air day after day, week after week. It takes time and disciplined effort to write books—to prepare for television tapings and messages delivered at services.

"The only bad thing that I could see about Kathryn was that she had an inability to work with some men. I think she respected my ministry,"

Dave Wilkerson said, "but not my management. She respected men of God, that's true, but she believed a good women could outdo at least seven men!

"Kathryn was a lot like Booth of the Salvation Army. Booth was a bellowing man when he wanted to see the work of God go ahead. He was impatient with people who couldn't do the work of God (the way he wanted it done or thought it should be done). I say, Kathryn was a good deal like him in this respect.

"Kathryn would put eighteen hours a day in and if anybody couldn't keep up with her she'd get impatient with them. I think at times she must have almost killed all of her staff off because no one could really keep pace with her. . . . I couldn't keep up with her."

I wondered about Kathryn Kuhlman's social life and asked her, "What of your social life? Are you able to have any close personal friends?"

"No, I'm a loner. No, no, I have no social life," she quickly replied. "No one will ever understand how alone I am. But it has to be that way. That's the reason I am a loner. *It must be.* I could have one of the greatest social lives of anyone in the world," she added, and explained, "because I am invited to the homes of some of the most famous people in the world, but I just don't go, y'know."

I related this to David Wilkerson. "It's really quite true," he acknowledged. "Just like a family has squabbles," Dave explained. "Well, her friends and co-workers were her family."

Kathryn may not have wanted to admit these frailties existed in her personality, but exist they did for she was, after all, human.

David Wilkerson and I agreed that you can't write a book or share about a person until you show that they are, indeed, human. "Kathryn was very, very human. But I think that's one of the things I admired about her," he said. "It gave me hope that I could be used of God with all my human frailties. So many of the books written about people are whitewashed. Don't do that with the story of Kathryn Kuhlman. You will be doing her a great injustice. You will be doing her Lord an injustice."

The Apostle Peter's many failures powerfully demonstrate that God can lift *us* from failure to new heights of usefulness for Him. Kathryn saw it, knew it, identified, and it encouraged her.

One of Kathryn's frailties had to do with her age. How old was she? It was a closely guarded secret. At the time of her death she was sixty-eight.

"I wish she'd have been open about her age," said one of her most loyal workers. "I think it would have added to her stature rather than detract. Up until the last year of her life in particular she did not look her age. It was a tribute to God's love for her that He kept her so youthful looking."

Jane Jones (dependable Shrine worker) said, "Kathryn was always just herself. She was dynamic and demonstrative. She surely was relaxed and at ease with the different people she interviewed. Although some did not like the way she did her hair or the clothes she wore, sometimes the stage would be glorified under the power of God and she would look like an angel or a young girl with arms outstretched toward heaven in her long, white dress. . . ."

What was the secret to her youthful appearance for so many years? Someone close to her revealed that she took vitamins with regularity, as well as wheat germ and honey. Someone else said they thought she spent half her life fasting and praying.

The speculation about Kathryn's age continued over the years. She made a definite point of informing the local Community Betterment Association of her hometown (who were working to gather information for the marker to erect on Main Street, Concordia) that her birth date was *not* to go on the marker. I saw the letter. Whether she was alive or whether she would be dead by the time the Committee decided, she was emphatic in asking that this information be kept classified!

" 'Vanity of vanities, saith the Preacher, vanity of vanities; all is vanity . . .' "[26] quoted Alfred Schlapper, the congenial town patriarch as we discussed Concordia's most famous personality.

"I remember when Kathryn came to Concordia for her mother's funeral in 1958. She filled the little Baptist church with flowers. There were flowers end-to-end, wall-to-wall. Kathryn came in wearing a great big lace-covered black hat," he reminisced.

"But she was a city girl now," spoke up Rudi rushing to her defense. It was Rudi Plaut speaking, the one and only Jewish person in the town of Concordia.

"I remember that funeral very well," said Ralph Erdwin. (Ralph's wife and Kathryn Kuhlman were first cousins.) "Kathryn was jubilant. . . ."

"That's beautiful," Rudi cried out. "Beautiful! If we are really godly people then we should be jubilant at someone's death, if that someone knew God, and I'm sure Mrs. Kuhlman did."

Rudi was obviously more of a newcomer to the Concordia scene than the others. "Let me teach you a good Jewish word," Rudi said. "It's *Kaddish*—that's the Jewish word for the prayer said in memory of the dead, and in that prayer we do not grieve, but we remember the soul, the good, the faith, and we are to continue living; we are not to mourn the dead. That's what Kathryn was doing."

Right then and there I decided that Kathryn would have liked Rudi Plaut and I told him so. He was pleased. "Would she? Is that so?" he said with a surprised look on his face.

"Yes, Rudi, whatever faults she may have had—and I'm sure you've heard about them through the years—Kathryn Kuhlman would have embraced you with love."

"You see, Rudi," my husband interjected, "Jesus was a Jew, as you know, and Kathryn had a great love for the Jewish people, just as we do."

"Well," he said, "she can be forgiven for being secretive about her age. There are worse things than that that a person can have wrong about them. . . ."

"It's a woman's prerogative not to reveal her age," I reminded all of them.

"In her looks Kathryn resembled her mother," Cousin Ralph related. "Her mother had red hair also. But she was tall like her father and like her Grandpa Walkenhorst."

Her hair! "Why didn't she do something different with her hair?" my beauty operator groaned. The same question had been voiced to me by other women. *Time* magazine in their September 14, 1970, issue described her as wearing her hair in a 1945 Shirley Temple hairdo.

There were those for whom this presented no problem in her appearance, like her childhood friend, Fern (Kroencke) Cullom who said, "When I saw her in 1972 in Kansas City she still had that beautiful red head of hair. I always envied her all those beautiful red curls as a child, and she still had them!"

Catherine Nixon Cooke, writing in *Coronet* magazine, remembers Kathryn's lamenting her red hair. "Whenever I went out with Mama, I had to wear a bonnet to hide my red hair. . . ."

Catherine Nixon Cooke went on to explain her reaction to seeing Kathryn Kuhlman at a miracle service. "Her oratory skill is an interesting combination of dramatics, humor, and humanness. Dressed in a long white dress, her red hair now looks beautiful. . . ."[27]

Her clothes? Exquisite gowns for her television appearances. "The lady likes fine clothes," *Time* magazine observed.

The Pittsburgh Press quoted writer Ann Butler in "Roto" as saying, "Miss Kuhlman struts out into the beige-toned vestibule of the church (First Presbyterian Church of Pittsburgh), glittering like the superstar she knows she has become.

"She looks chic in a classic tan knit sheath, stylish suede platform sandals, and bronze drop earrings."[28]

If Kathryn Kuhlman had looked dowdy and dressed unattractively what would the media have said? Quite possibly the same people who criticized her for the beautiful clothes she liked, and the way she dressed, would have been among those finding fault with her if she had dressed in an unfashionable way.

And so she always dressed beautifully, often in a flowing gown of a soft, chiffonlike fabric that draped about her in lovely swirling folds. This may not have been quite what some expected from a woman evangelist, but then those same people might not have approved of John the Baptist either, who came wearing strange garb, no doubt looking more like a wild man from the wilderness than the prophetic forerunner of Christ! Many early Christian leaders were a bit unorthodox in their approach and attire, my research has revealed. Kathryn Kuhlman was no exception.

You never learn faith and trust in easy circumstances. Whatever frailties she had—and she knew she had them—Kathryn knew also, because she'd learned firsthand—the hard way—that you can safely leave the problems and obstructions to God and just concentrate on His instructions, and when you do, you are assured of answers and help. Real faith is always anchored in the Word. Kathryn Kuhlman was first and foremost a woman of the Word.

14
Kathryn the Person

. . . touch not mine anointed, and do my prophets no harm.

Psalms 105:15 KJV

KATHRYN'S PRIVATE life—her every move and whim—was subject to scrutiny from outsiders.

She could not be faulted for guarding against the invasion of her privacy as much as possible. Considering the worldwide attention she attracted, it is amazing that she was able, to a remarkable degree, to maintain a certain mystique so that many areas of her life and personality could not be the subject of a curious writer's pen. I could understand why her personal life remained, for the most part, quite unknown. She was adept at answering interviewers' questions, revealing in part, but never quite in whole. The charisma—the mystery—grew, as a result, through the years. It wasn't that she was being unresponsive, but it was her ability to turn the conversation back to the work God had given her to do.

When Kathryn Kuhlman emphasized that she was a "very private person," she meant just that. Her life was so radically different after receiving the infilling of the Holy Spirit and the outpouring of that power, that events from earlier periods in her life receded into the back of her mind in a more than normal way. There are those who insist this was a deliberate ploy in order to "cover up" for her past. But I wonder how many readers would want every detail of *their* pasts dragged out for public scrutiny? And so this presented Kathryn the person with some difficulties, for there were always those seeking to discredit the ministry through calling attention to what they felt were her glaring shortcomings.

Some writers, like Allen Spraggett, understood this dichotomy in her life. In his estimation she was not evasive.

He found her to be disarmingly candid about certain aspects of her life (her educational inadequacies, for example). What she left unsaid contributed to the aura that surrounded her ministry and she knew better than to tamper with what God was doing.

How did Kathryn Kuhlman handle her emotions? Did she ever cry? Womanlike, did she give in to her feelings? Women, it is generally admitted, are more emotional than men. Or was Kathryn Kuhlman a rare exception?

Christianity Today in its March 12, 1976, issue reported that in August of 1975 when Kathryn Kuhlman looked out at her audience at Melodyland Christian Center in Anaheim, California, she said: "Some of you will never know what I'm talking about." Her eyes glistened and a tear spilled onto her cheek. "To have peace with God," she said, "one must intentionally die to self, to all self ambition, until you are only living for Jesus."[29]

There were reporters and writers who made mention of the fact that they saw tears in Kathryn Kuhlman's eyes on several occasions. She knew how to weep with those who wept. "You cannot feel for someone else in their sorrow unless you've had it," she told us.

The tears glistening in her eyes the day she spoke at Anaheim Melodyland Christian Center were caused by what one person very close to her ministry has said was "the heartbreak, the crush of her life." It had to do with the problems she encountered in connection with a $430,000 lawsuit filed against her by a former business manager. (That lawsuit was settled out of court.) This, however, was a stunning blow to her and "observers close to Miss Kuhlman said that her health suddenly deteriorated about the time the allegations came to the attention of the press and that afterward she was not the same emotionally."[30]

I am led to believe that Kathryn Kuhlman shed many tears. Alone, hugging her pillow at night, with no one's shoulder to cry on, this woman, capable of such depth of emotion, must surely have cried. Yes, she had her beloved "Maggie," whom she herself referred to as her secretary-phone-answerer-letter-writer-fellow-minister, loyal friend. And there were others who had been at her side for over twenty-five years. But the loneliness that cries out for human companionship on the physical level is very real, and Kathryn Kuhlman was very much a woman.

"What about women today going into this kind of work?" I asked her.

"There is a price to pay before I slip into that long white dress and appear on stage," she softly whispered. "Consecration." She whispered the word again, "Consecration. This is really a man's work. I work hard, sometimes seventeen or eighteen hours a day. I get little sleep. I stand at the pulpit four-and-a-half hours at a time without sitting down once, and I can still leave the stage as refreshed as when I walked on. I have given myself completely to the Holy Spirit, and He gives me strength and sustenance—all that I need.

"I'd give anything if I could have just been a good housewife, a good cook. And I'd like to have had a big family. It would have been nice to have a man boss me around.

"Let women be sure—very sure—that they have a call from God before they ever decide to enter such a ministry," was her admonition. "If you are not definitely called, don't do it."

What of Kathryn Kuhlman's home? Where did she live? Readers would want to know and so I asked her about where Kathryn the person is when she's not at a miracle service.

"I have a home which I bought in 1948 in Fox Chapel, Pittsburgh. It is a ranch-style house. It was almost all country then with deer and rabbits running about. But it has grown up about it since then. But do you realize I'm there to sleep sometimes not more than three nights a month! I'm sure people don't realize that I'm on the go constantly. I average 400,000 to 500,000 air miles a year."

Dave Wilkerson said that she also had an apartment where he and his wife stayed when they were in Pittsburgh, one that she kept just for guests. "It was furnished in very beautiful antiques. When we first went in I was afraid I'd knock over some piece of Oriental art. But this was her hobby—decorating places. And in her travels around the world she took time out to roam about looking for these antiques. Sure that took time, she wasn't praying all the time. Who does? But she actually spent less time at that than a husband and wife do in caring for one another and each other's needs. Kathryn Kuhlman's hobby was antiques.

"After she started having regular services in California," Dave said, "she got an apartment in Newport Beach. It, too, was very beautiful. It had Kathryn's touch. One word describes it: *class!* But she was not what you could call extravagant; she just had this certain class.

"Neither did she ever flaunt what she had; and she gave away far, far more than she ever kept for herself. She was very careful who came into her places and she never talked about them. I tried to get her to, but she wouldn't do it. It seemed so incongruous to me—sitting there in her beautiful apartment among all those antiques, yet she wanted only to talk about the Lord."

Kathryn Kuhlman had revealed to me her appreciation for fine art objects. I asked her what she did for recreation. "Is a woman in your position able to have satisfying hobbies or diversion of some kind?"

Laughter. Deep-throated laughter and a twinkle in her eyes as she responded. "I've never played golf or any such things, although, mind you, I don't fault those who do. But a day of rest and doing nothing seems such a wasted day for me. I love what I do and anything else is so mediocre really. But one thing I like, and one thing I can do—I can completely release my mind with antiques. I just love antiques so I will go into these stores and just wander around because I appreciate art. Now when I'm talking about antiques, I'm not talking about broken-down furniture; I'm not talking about that kind of 'art.'

"But I admire a person who is an artist in any field, and I just love seeing the work of someone else, y' know. But that's the only hobby I really have. . . ."

David Wilkerson's conversation only confirmed what Kathryn Kuhlman herself had already revealed to me. Someone else might call this "materialistic lust." But this was Kathryn the person. The same people who would fault her for enjoying art treasures might think nothing of owning a camper truck with a boat tied on behind and all the fishing gear and camping paraphernalia besides. Or someone else might "indulge" in the finest golf clubs and think nothing of spending every weekend and holiday on the golf course. Another person might have an expensive hobby of photography. Many comparisons could be drawn—one man's idea of luxury, "materialistic lusts," and "indulgence," would not be considered as such by another person.

"You could never outgive Kathryn Kuhlman." Many people said this over and over again, including David Wilkerson who shared his insights —not to call attention to what some might consider Kathryn's weaknesses—but because it only pointed up the fact that she was a human being whom God touched and used. "She had a divine call from God. She was an institution. There will never be another like her," Dave said with deep feeling. "But the very fact that she was so human was a great encouragement to me and would be, I believe, to readers."

In no way should new insights into Kathryn the person diminish her in the eyes of the reader. We need to hear once again the words of the Apostle Paul: "For he [God] saith to Moses, I will have mercy . . . and I will have compassion on whom I will have compassion. So then it is not of him that willeth, nor of him that runneth, but of God that sheweth mercy."[31]

I asked Kathryn about her traveling. "Do you have traveling companions?"

"I travel alone an awful lot," she said. "I meet the most interesting people that way!" She didn't try to disguise herself. She took delight in telling about the airplane pilot, for instance, or stewardess, who upon recognizing her identity would pull out a copy of one of her books and say, "Look what I just happen to be reading!"

"What about those early years? Did she ever talk about them to you?" I questioned Dave Wilkerson.

"I can answer that best by telling you that she really didn't want to leave Pittsburgh after she once got established so well there, and I think it was for fear someone would dig up her past.

"No, I don't know anything about those early years.

"But Pittsburgh was something else—she had a protected island. There she had overcome the criticism; the press had learned to live with her. I wanted her to go to Los Angeles and it took some urging. For a long time she persistently said *no*. But I think she thought if she went to Los Angeles and other places she'd have to go through it all again. She had already fought that battle and settled it in Pittsburgh. It was a very secure haven."

We discussed the admonition of the Lord as given in Psalms 105:15: "Touch not mine anointed, and do my prophets no harm."

Dave commented: "Those people who touched her [with an eye to hurting her and discrediting her ministry] are on very dangerous ground. I have never seen anyone 'touch God's anointed' and get away with it."

Of herself Kathryn said to us, "People can attack me personally, if they wish. I don't care what anyone calls me. I don't mind one bit what they say, but don't attack the power of God. You are on dangerous ground when you attack God, Jesus Christ, and the Holy Spirit. Remember, the Bible needs no defense. God needs no defense. Divine healing in the body needs no defense. Divine healing is as old as God."

15

"God Didn't Call Me to Build Buildings"

Let love be your greatest aim. . . .

1 Corinthians 14:1

"I COULD NEVER UNDERSTAND how Kathryn Kuhlman's staff could do all they did out of their four little rooms in the Carlton House [Pittsburgh hotel]," a friend of hers observed. "Eventually she added a couple more rooms, but even then, the facilities were unbelievably small in comparison to some Christian organizations that did not have the outreach of the Kathryn Kuhlman Foundation."

We were discussing the physical layout of the Foundation headquarters in Pittsburgh, Pennsylvania.

"Once when I commented about this to her, she said to me, 'I don't want to be bogged down with big headquarters. God didn't call me to build buildings, set up big offices, and have a huge staff.'"

In this regard Kathryn Kuhlman successfully avoided what someone has described as "the curse of many religious organizations—the growth syndrome where bigger is supposedly better."

The staff at the Pittsburgh Foundation office was kept to a minimum. "Kathryn Kuhlman did not have this thing about the more staff you have as being a badge of success with herself as the authority figure. The staff did a fantastic job—these were dedicated, trusted people." The tribute was well deserved.

Her offices in Newport Beach and Hollywood, California, were considered "much nicer" to quote another friend.

"But even those offices were also manned by what would have to be considered a skeleton staff. She believed in having a few people who were well paid and who really fit the slot.

"Bringing people in for the sake of numbers was not a hang-up with her. The people who surrounded her had found a place of total effectiveness—a call of God. The result was 'peace in the family.' "

David Wilkerson credits much of his own effectiveness to many things he learned from Kathryn Kuhlman. "She pointed to other ministries who had big headquarters and beautiful buildings with huge staffs and oversized mailing lists, and she'd smile and say, 'Isn't it amazing, David, we just have a few workers and rented offices, but our budget is just as high, we're doing just as much—and I don't have the headaches.' "

This was not criticism necessarily on her part toward those who found it necessary to function this way—but it was not *her* way and she was simply pointing out the difference. "Yet the Kathryn Kuhlman Foundation had a worldwide pulpit," Dave pointed out.

There will undoubtedly be special rewards in heaven for the loyal people who surrounded Kathryn Kuhlman.

"Kathryn definitely had loyalty from these people," Dave Wilkerson said. "Loyalty was a number one prerequisite with her. Before talent or anything else, there was this matter of loyalty which she rightfully insisted upon.

"I tell the people who come to work for our organization the thing I learned from Kathryn, and that is: we pattern ourselves just like Gideon [in the Bible]. She told her co-workers exactly what Gideon told the army he assembled, 'We fight for God and for Gideon!' Kathryn said, 'You go against the enemy with the sword of the Lord and with Kathryn Kuhlman.' This was ingrained in me, and I saw that kind of loyalty in her offices. When they saw that she was right, they joined her in standing against the critical world. They became a hedge against criticism for her. Much of the criticism leveled against her was taken by these people. Much of it, I'm certain, she didn't hear because of their loyalty. It is vital to those of us who are in the Lord's work that we have people like that surrounding us."

From the Pittsburgh and California offices a worldwide ministry was carried on that received far less publicity than the actual miracle services, though in scope and in terms of outreach effectiveness their importance cannot be measured.

Dave Wilkerson explained her concern this way: "I think it's a law of God in operation: give and ye shall receive. The more she gave, the more she received. I remember once when we needed a building on our Teen Challenge Farm that she came down and ministered and gave fifty thousand dollars. I said to her at the time, 'Now how in the world do I thank you?'

"Her answer was quick, 'Look, don't thank me. I've been spending this past week trying to figure out what God's going to do here . . . I'm trying to figure out how to handle God's blessings. You just pray that I'll be able to withstand the onslaught of blessing. I've learned a long time ago that you have to prepare for God's blessings, you know, you can't outgive Him. Just pray that God will help us at the Foundation to handle our end of it.'

"She gave to our Teen Challenge work over the years about $200 thousand. She came to New York City and walked the streets with us. Nicky Cruz took her up into the areas where there was a concentration of our efforts. She went up into these kids' hideouts and saw them shooting drugs; she went into all these areas because she wanted to see personally what was happening. She wanted to get the burden for it. She spent at least two full days just walking up through Harlem and out through those hell holes. But she flew into New York specifically for that purpose—to walk the streets so she would know firsthand.

"I remember going with her into one room that had about thirty prostitutes and drug addicts. She walked around among them, like she was in a healing service, just laying hands on them, and praying for them. Three or four of them got saved and really went on with the Lord and came into our Teen Challenge program. But she was so perceptive about people, even these kids.

"I once saw her set one of my workers down and talk to him about how to keep his ministry straight. She did it out of love. She sat down with me a number of times and never hesitated to tell you when she thought you were going off one way or the other [off center from your call].

"When it came time for our Teen Challenge Twentieth-Anniversary

Banquet, she was there. When she came in I remember her saying to me, 'Dave, I'm so tired . . . I don't think I can really preach tonight.' My heart went out to her and I said, 'Don't try to. Just talk a little bit from your heart.' And that's what she did. She was very demonstrative and yes, dramatic, and I felt a bit embarrassed about everything she said —but do you know, just her being there helped us so tremendously. She put that banquet and our goals way over the top.

"When I finally stopped working with her (the monthly meetings), it was because I felt that I had become too dependent on the financial help she was giving us. I was more or less depending on the five thousand dollars or ten thousand dollars a month the Foundation was giving us, and I couldn't discern my motives—was I going for the money? We needed it so much in those early days of the Teen Challenge work; or what were my reasons? And also, I found that time-wise I was getting too busy. I had been very involved with her services for almost three years. But she made it clear that if we ever needed money for the work to come and see her. What she did for us was quite typical of her love and concern for the Lord's work."

No, Kathryn Kuhlman did not feel called to build buildings for her own Foundation work, but she knew the importance of con-tributing to others who were in the forefront of ministering—for in-stance, to youth. She helped to build lives. Through its Scholarship Fund and Revolving Loan Fund, the Kathryn Kuhlman Foundation provided many scholarships to more than a dozen colleges. The Foundation has contributed to a wide variety of charitable organiza-tions in this country and overseas.

The St. Louis Post Dispatch reported that since 1948 at least two million people had been healed and their lives touched through the Kathryn Kuhlman ministry, but that ministry was more far-reaching than the average individual realized. There was also the wide-flung impact of her radio and television shows. The radio broadcasts covered most of the nation, five-days-a-week, thirty-minute programs; and over-seas broadcasts reached most of Europe, Northern Africa, and behind the Iron Curtain, with short-wave broadcasts to Australia and from Bogota, South America. For more than eight years her weekly television shows throughout the United States and Canada attracted the interest of millions.

Then there are her three books: *I Believe In Miracles* (best-seller, more than 2 million copies sold); *God Can Do It Again* (another best-seller); and *Nothing Is Impossible With God.* There were also four small "companion books": *Captain Le Vrier Believes in Miracles; 10,000 Miles for a Miracle; How Big Is God?* and *Standing Tall.*

Translations of these books have been made in more than thirteen foreign languages, and some of her books are in Braille transcript.

Twenty-two mission stations had been erected overseas and each was presented debt-free to the native people as a gift from the Foundation.

She had a way of assessing needs and then setting about to help solve them without fuss or fanfare. "She was always looking for ways to give things to others," Dave Wilkerson and several others related. "She enjoyed buying clothes for people. Her vision was not so far-reaching that she forgot the needy at her own doorstep."

"Much was given out of her own pocket," someone else said.

"I think she enjoyed giving from her missionary Samaritan bag. But she never forgot where this money originally came from—God's people.

"I rather believe she went around challenging the Lord, 'I've got this money, these bills, Lord. Where do You want them to go?' "

Dave Wilkerson and Nicky Cruz (and others) remember that Kathryn Kuhlman bought them their first tailor-made suits. This she did out of her own pocket—from that Samaritan bag!

Love is something you do was her philosophy. She had come a long way in her primitive travels across country to preach in out-of-the-way places—riding the buses and trains (when she could afford that), or driving an inexpensive-model car. No longer did she have to rely on the goodness of someone's heart to open up their home for her and her pianist to provide a night's lodging, or later to stay in a cheap hotel. But she had not forgotten those days. Her heart told her that as a wise steward of money God's people had given—many of them sacrificially—she should put those gifts to good use. And that she did.

Dan Malachuk, publisher of the *National Courier,* asked Miss Kuhlman one time, "Will you ever build a large church as part of a memorial for people to remember you?"

She had replied, "No, God called me to minister to people, not buildings. The people will live on to continue the ministry. I don't want any buildings to substitute for where God's glory really is—in people."[32]

16
Kathryn's Faith

He staggered not at the promise of God through unbelief, but
was strong in faith, giving glory to God.

Romans 4:20 KJV

"I AM THE MOST unlikely person in the world for God to choose to use for His instrument. All I have is my love and my faith."

It was enough. Enough for anyone who wants to be used of God. It was enough for Kathryn Kuhlman!

Despite all efforts of self-effacement, Kathryn Kuhlman was a remarkable woman whose achievements stagger one's thinking whether one was in agreement with her or not.

"For years I had a complex because I've got no degrees or seminary training," she often explained. "All I know is what I've learned as I've watched the Holy Spirit at work."

It was more than adequate to equip her for the work God called her to do!

But Kathryn Kuhlman did have two honorary doctor degrees. One she'd had for many years; the other, an Honorary Doctor of Humane Letters was awarded by Oral Roberts University, Tulsa, Oklahoma, in May, 1972. In actuality, however, she was an ordained minister of the Gospel.

Another writer described her as being both keen-minded and, if the occasion requires, tough-minded. "It would be a mistake to think of Kathryn Kuhlman as intellectually dull. She is about as dull as a rapier. I have often thought, as I watched her: 'This woman is nobody's fool.' "[33]

"Sometimes . . . sometimes I feel so *stoo-pid,*" she was heard to say frequently.

With regard to the way she referred to herself as being "stupid," and "ordinary," Dave Wilkerson observed: "She came across as being very naïve (particularly about financial matters). But she was a brilliant person able to discern real human need. Being naïve was a part of her whole makeup. I've seen her really light into people who thought she was just a 'dumb evangelist.' She'd sit there listening and saying, 'Yes, yes, yes,' and then she'd cut them down to size. She could read someone off almost like she'd read their mind. We've all seen her do this on television with someone who was attempting to show her up.

"Actually though, she didn't let enough of the human aspect of her life come across. I cheered her more one day when I saw her on the Dick Cavett show. Dick had it all set up; *he* was going to rip Kathryn Kuhlman apart (so he thought!). But she was so brilliant when 'cornered.' I remember the incident very well. I was watching TV with my wife, and I just jumped up and down, cheering and yelling, saying, 'Give it to him!' It was the first time I'd ever seen Dick Cavett without words. The drummer in his band had been to her meetings and gotten healed. Dick was saying, 'Well, I've never met anyone who has been to your meetings,' and she turned and said, 'Why don't you talk to your drummer!'

"Nobody—but I mean nobody—could ever get the best of Kathryn Kuhlman!"

Kathryn may have considered herself unlearned and stupid in some respects, but deep down in her heart she knew that God could take care of her every deficiency and she could depend on Him. But she also did have a very healthy self-respect.

Dan L. Thrapp, former Religion Editor of the *Los Angeles Times*, wrote of Miss Kuhlman, February 16, 1970: "Whether you agree this vibrant Pittsburgh gospel preacher is a great evangelist and healer, or whether you think her ministry is for the gullible—or the birds—she is a genuine phenomenon."[34] He backed up his statements with firsthand observations of her and a meeting in the Los Angeles Shrine Auditorium.

Miss Kuhlman regretted the emphasis of the media. "The news media dwells on the spectacular—the miracle healings—when really the transformation of a life, the salvation of a soul is something eternal and spiritual healing is far greater. A person's greatest possession is his faith in God."

I listened carefully to a TV talk-show interview when a caller pleaded with Miss Kuhlman to allow her to bring her desperately sick child to a service and for her to lay her hands on this precious daughter. Kathryn Kuhlman, with pain written all over her sensitive face that day, reminded the woman that the child could be healed right at home just as easily as in a miracle service. "Don't reach out and touch Kathryn Kuhlman, reach up and touch God. People come to the services because there is a oneness in the Spirit, and when you join with thousands who are in prayer it is so much easier to pray and to believe God. But keep your eyes on Jesus, wherever you are."

She preached no theology of healing. She reached the point where she no longer even believed that faith necessarily earned someone a healing, or that lack of faith forbade it. She had seen too many nonbelievers cured and too many believers go away still in wheelchairs or sick. "It is *all* the sovereign act of God," she would explain tirelessly.

Christianity Today, in its extensive interview, asked her to comment regarding her personal feelings about those who came to the meetings and went away without having been healed. Her reply: "Whether or not someone is healed is in the hands of God. At no time was it my responsibility. But I'm human, and you'll never know how I hurt on the inside when I see those who came in wheelchairs being pushed into the street again. You'll never know the ache, the suffering I feel, but the answer I must leave with God. . . . No, I do not know why all are not healed physically, but all *can* be healed spiritually, and that's the greatest miracle any human being can know."[35]

It may have been in part because she had no children of her own that Kathryn Kuhlman was always deeply moved when children received a miracle touch from God and were healed in one of the great miracle services. But her own faith was so real that she strongly identified with the demonstration of childlike faith on the part of these little ones. Three of the Gospel writers relate the story of Jesus drawing to Himself a little child and then giving the beautiful story of the need to have a childlike faith.

In children she saw the perfect faith about which Jesus spoke and which He honored time after time after time. Kathryn herself possessed that kind of faith.

She knew that prayer and faith worked harmoniously together, and that both were necessary in their distinct functions, yet quite different in their nature. She said, "Prayer is the voice of the soul, while faith is the hand. It is only through prayer that the soul can establish communion with its Creator, and it is only through faith that spiritual victories are won.

"Prayer knocks at the door of grace, while faith opens it. Prayer contacts God, while faith obtains an audience. Prayer makes a petition, while faith presses through the multitudes to touch the Hem of His Garment, and receives from His giving Hand. Prayer quotes the promise, while faith boldly proclaims the fulfillment of that promise. . . .

"The greatest power that God has given to men and women, is the power of prayer, but always remember, God has established the law of prayer and faith. Prayer is conscious of the need, while faith supplies it."[36]

Of the dynamics of prayer she said: "There is a spiritual force released when people's hearts are united. The glory falls when a group, in the words of the Book of Acts, 'are all with one accord in one place.' I have nothing to do with this. It's their own power in prayer, their oneness in the Spirit."[37]

If there was one thing Kathryn Kuhlman had learned through the years, it was the absolute necessity of looking beyond human resources to the One who made the promises recorded in the Word. She knew that human limitation is *not* the point of divine limitation. How much she must have identified with Abraham of old! (*See* Romans 4:18–24.)

"There is a tragic dearth of faith in the world today," she would say. "Creeds, traditions, opinions—all these have taken the place in the hearts of men—even many professing to be Christians—of that kind of faith the Bible speaks of that 'moves mountains.' And we are living in a time that, more than ever, needs to have that kind of believing faith, living faith in Jesus Christ.

"Faith is always Christ-centered, if it is Bible faith. I regret the confusion that exists, again even in the ranks of believers, about what faith is, and what faith does.

"Can you remember that faith is simply the heart moving toward Jesus, and receiving from Him.

"Faith is the latchstring to God's great Supply House.

"And we need to seek it. Faith *is* to be sought, 'For unto you it is given,' the Word declares. You don't work faith up . . . faith comes down . . . it is the active moving of the Holy Spirit in believing exercise. Faith is *from* God, in Jesus' Name, anointed by the Third Person."

She liked to tell people to read the story of the woman in the New Testament who exercised such believing faith that she said, "If I can but touch the hem of His garment, I shall be made whole."[38]

"What an expression of faith that was!" Kathryn Kuhlman said. "This woman had an overwhelming need of the Lord's help. Her consuming thought was for the healing of her body. She was desperate. She did not approach Jesus with the idea that *if* He healed her, it would be wonderful, but she approached Him with her whole heart and mind, as well as with her poor, disease-wracked body. She had no other hope. It was Jesus and Jesus only. It wasn't easy for her to reach Him; the press of the crowd was great. *The one sure way to get by the people who stand between you and Jesus is to get on your knees.* Press through, Beloved, press through. That is the way to touch the Lord. Notice that she did not tug at Him, she merely touched Him! What it all means is that Lydia was reaching out to the Son of God. Jesus' words to her are for us as well, 'Daughter, thy faith hath made thee whole; go in peace, and be whole . . .'

"The issue is whether or not we shall take God at His Word."

Loraine (LeVrier) Geers whose father, Capt. John LeVrier, was miraculously healed of cancer, attended ten of Kathryn Kuhlman's miracle services since February 21, 1971 (the date her father was healed). "Because my own daddy was the first person to be miraculously healed

I really had an unusual introduction to Kathryn Kuhlman. But most amazing to me was the part of her service when everyone was singing, hands held high in the air, praising and worshiping the Lord and she would say, 'Whatever you want from the Lord, just receive it. Right now, just receive whatever you need.'

"Not everyone there received whatever they wanted or needed, but isn't it simply amazing that anyone could have that much faith? In the words of *Reader's Digest*, Kathryn Kuhlman has got to be 'The Most Unforgettable Character I Ever Met.' I never saw anyone with so much faith."

Kathryn Kuhlman's faith was like that of a little, trusting child. "Dear God," she prayed, "give to us the simple faith that little children know —the faith to believe in the living Person and Power of Jesus: the faith to look for Miracles upon this earth below. For if we wear this simple faith wrapped like a cloak around us, we will be blessed as children are, and it is then that we will not only know ABOUT LIFE—we will know HOW TO LIVE LIFE!"[39]

17
In Journeyings Often

I have traveled many weary miles. . . . I have lived with
weariness and pain and sleepless nights. . . .
                                                    2 Corinthians 11:26, 27

SHE HAD A GLOBULAR interdenominational following of millions. Wherever she went—from Youngstown, Ohio to Tel Aviv, Israel—crowds
overflowed into the streets for blocks around, waiting, hoping to get into
the huge auditoriums. They jam-packed the buildings—the sick, the
anguished, the faithful and the curious.

Energetically and effectively she pursued the ministry into which she
had been thrust, and hundreds of thousands were constantly refreshed
by the manifestations of God's power. It was simple faith which compelled her to go, like the Apostle Paul, who wrote to the Corinthian
Christians explaining what was happening in his ministry. How easily
she could have echoed the apostle's words: "I have traveled many weary
miles. . . . I have lived with weariness and pain and sleepless nights."
In the early days of her ministry she could have also picked up the
apostle's words: ". . . Often I have been hungry and thirsty and have
gone without food; often I have shivered with cold, without enough
clothing to keep me warm."[40]

Kathryn had trustingly placed her hand in the hand of the Lord; she
followed, unafraid, into whatever pathway He led. Little did she know
it would lead her to crisscross the nation hundreds of times, and take
her across the oceans.

The Apostle Paul knew what it was to have himself and his ministry
called into question by the religious leaders of his day and the organized
Church. Kathryn could share in that experience. She, like Paul, had a
deep concern for the Church.

Knowing full well that there were those in her audiences who were critical and skeptical, she would speak in what was almost an aside to them. With all the earnestness she possessed she would bare her soul, pleading for them to open themselves up to the reality of the Holy Ghost and His power to work on their behalf.

Early in her ministry she discovered that she had no one to whom she could turn, nowhere else to go, other than to God's Word. "As I sought, I saw for the very first time that there was more than God the Father and more than Him giving Jesus Christ. Sure I had learned it early— John 3:16. But something else had happened before God gave His Son . . . It would have to take sinless blood to secure man's salvation.

"Before God gave His Son, before Jesus consented to come, He offered Himself first through the Holy Spirit. We fail to see this some- times. I often think of those who try to minimize the power of the Holy Spirit. If Jesus could trust Him, if Jesus staked everything He had on the Holy Spirit, then you and I can also. Jesus had faith, Jesus had confidence in Him . . . Jesus was just as dependent as you and I are on the Holy Spirit. That is the reason why when Jesus went back to glory again, He left the Church the most glorious Gift.

"We are the gift that the Father gave to His Son. That is the reason Jesus, when talking to the Father, said, 'These that thou has given to me.' And just before Jesus went away He wanted to give to the Church the greatest Gift He could give to His own, the ones who had been so faithful and true to Him—and that's why He said, 'But ye shall receive power, after that the Holy Ghost is come upon you. . . .'[41]

"Oh, I wish I could climb the highest mountaintop, I wish I could shout it until every man who stands behind the pulpit, every priest, every rabbi, every minister could know, hear, understand, believe it, and re- ceive Him—this wonderful Gift that Jesus gave to His Church, this body of believers. It is a sacred Gift, a holy Gift, no greater Gift could Jesus give. God the Father had given Him the body of believers; Jesus, in turn, wanted to give this body a Gift. What greater Gift could He have given!

"Do you know the glorious strengthening power of the Holy Spirit? The Apostle Paul did. Jesus knew the power and the Presence of the Holy Spirit. Jesus had the courage; Jesus had what it takes when the hour came when He had to yield . . . Jesus understood . . . Jesus knew the secret of His earthly victory, and that was the reason, in His last bequest He said, 'And ye shall receive power . . .'—the same power He had manifest in His life here upon earth.

"Don't you see it?" she questioned, as she looked out over those vast auditoriums filled to overflowing with those who she knew were so hungry for the truth. "It changed my life; it changed my ministry. . . . This ministry is what it is today because of the power of the Holy Ghost—the power of the Holy Spirit. How better can I tell you?" she implored with outstretched hands, her voice straining with every ounce of energy she possessed.

"Turn it all over to the Holy Spirit—your self, your will. You will be a new man . . . you will be a new woman . . . you will get results," her voice was almost a whisper now. " 'And ye shall receive power, after that the Holy Ghost is come upon you,' " she repeated the Scripture.

"What happened on the Day of Pentecost? He came! The Holy Spirit came! We know that Jesus made it to heaven safely because the Holy Spirit arrived on schedule!

"Those were exciting times in the early Church. Today is still the Day of Pentecost and we have every right to have the same things happen in our churches as happened then. . . . I know the secret to the power in this ministry. I know the secret to those who are healed. The secret is found in the Person of the Holy Spirit. I have chosen to accept the Gift that Jesus left for me!"

The Holy Spirit at work in her was too powerful for mere man to comprehend. She could not understand it; people in the audience could not fathom it. How God could use one person in such an awe-inspiring way! But there was power—wonder-working power! The Word of God faithfully declares that on the Day of Pentecost as the onlookers saw what was happening they were stunned, amazed, and perplexed (*see* Acts 2). "A deep sense of awe was on them all, and the apostles did many miracles" (Acts 2:43). And this is the way it was wherever Kathryn Kuhlman went "in [her] journeyings often."

18
The Market Place

Wherever he went—in villages and cities, and out on the
farms—they laid the sick in the market plazas and streets,
and begged him to let them at least touch the fringes of his
clothes; and as many as touched him were healed.

Mark 6:56

IT WAS A BRIGHT but chilly Sunday morning, however it didn't keep the
crowd away. You could not see the entrance to the Shrine Auditorium
even at 9:30 A.M., so great was the crowd. By the time the miracle service
began, and the doors opened shortly before one o'clock, the crowd would
have swelled to such proportions that many were turned away. The
capacity of the auditorium was 7,500 people, but we were told that
sometimes twice that many tried to get in.

Our hearts ached as we walked past the long lines to the side entrance
where we had been directed. There were some on stretchers, pain etched
on their faces; a long line of wheelchair patients was being given immediate entrance at another side door. It was a place of hustle and bustle,
but all orderly.

Choir members and individuals with special badges were allowed early
entrance. Others, like myself, with letters in hand, were given admit-
tance. I took one last look at the crowd outside—people were sitting in
lawn chairs, one girl sat on a Foremost milk crate; it was an amazingly
diverse multitude. In the parking lot we had seen buses arriving marked
CHARTERED—they came from such faraway places as Portland, Oregon,
and even Las Vegas, Nevada.

The scene was not too unlike that which Jesus and the disciples
encountered as they went from city to city when He walked upon this
earth. The press of the crowd was always great (*see*, for instance, Mark
6:31, 34, 39, 54–56). I also envisioned a similar scene when the early

apostles preached and the sick were healed (*see* the Book of Acts). Later, inside the auditorium as the service was underway, I remembered what Jesus said: "Nevertheless, I tell you the truth; It is expedient for you that I go away: for if I go not away, the Comforter will not come unto you; but if I depart, I will send him unto you. . . ."42 The disciples were mystified, "Whatever is he saying? . . . We don't know what he means."43

We were seeing what Jesus meant! "When the Holy Spirit, who is truth, comes, he shall guide you into all truth, for he will not be presenting his own ideas, but will be passing on to you what he has heard. He will tell you about the future. He shall praise me and bring me great honor by showing you my glory."44

"I have learned to be obedient to the Holy Spirit. I cannot use the Holy Spirit; He only uses me. . . ." Kathryn Kuhlman was speaking. "You and I are personal to Him; the desires of our hearts are personal to Him. God sees you as an individual. We have delegations here today from all over the world . . . there is a Swedish delegation out there I'm told . . . others from Hawaii, Las Vegas, Oregon, and oh, yes, Captain LeVrier is here from Houston, Texas. . . .

"God is so real . . . Hebrews 13:8 tells us, 'Jesus Christ is the same yesterday, today, and forever.' I believe it; I know it. . . .

"If I live to be 120 I'll die wanting to please God and telling others of His mercy, His love, and His power. . . .

"We've gotten to the place where we just can't accept the supernatural. We are so mentally conditioned . . . we want to accept only that which is logical . . . but it is impossible to explain the work of the Holy Spirit. . . ." Her voice was barely audible, but all around one sensed that Power and that Presence of the Holy Spirit.

Now she was praying: "Would You please, loving Father, in Your tender mercy, trust these who have come with a healing. Wonderful Jesus, You can trust me . . . I vow to give You all the praise. . . .

"I rebuke that cancer in the mighty Name of Jesus—that asthmatic condition. . . .

"Oh, we are being given another early Church experience in this place today. . . . You have everything to gain and not one thing to lose when you trust God.

"We're not talking about faith now—we're seeing God's mercy," and indeed we were as the aisles were crowded with those claiming healings.

Kathryn Kuhlman stood back momentarily in amazement as the power continued to fall. It was a familiar scene to her—she'd seen miracles like this thousands of times in hundreds of places, yet she was just as amazed with each as though it had been the first one she'd ever experienced. "It isn't an act when I stand here awed," she explained. "I'm human too. I'm not a psychic healer. I don't believe that God has given me anything special that you can't have too. . . . Get your eyes off Kathryn Kuhlman. I beg of every person in this place, don't look to me. . . . I would like to slip behind the curtains. I'm only a mouthpiece telling you how big God is!" And the miracles continued. The Holy Spirit, working through her, was bringing God great glory.

One year and one month later I was once again in the Los Angeles Shrine Auditorium. Only this time it was for Kathryn Kuhlman's Memorial Service. The "market place" was again a place of hustle and bustle, but this occasion was more subdued. The general air of expectancy was somehow missing; yet there were those in wheelchairs and others who one sensed came hoping for a healing.

The choir was in its place—hundreds of men and women presenting a variegated mass of color. Missing was the aristocratic-looking white-maned choir director whom we'd seen the year before. Dr. Metcalfe, a distinguished musician with a doctor of philosophy degree from St. Olaf's, had been a part of the Kuhlman team for over twenty-six years. One year to the day of Dr. Metcalfe's death, Kathryn Kuhlman died. In his place was Paul Ferrin, himself a well-known musician, who had stepped into Dr. Metcalfe's vacancy at Kathryn's request. Also on the platform was Kathy Salazar, Paul Ferrin's daughter, named after Kathryn Kuhlman. Kathy is an accomplished harpist.

The service itself was a loving tribute to that one who had ministered with such love and humility through the years. A number of such services were held in various places across the country in the weeks that followed Miss Kuhlman's death. At each the choirs sang the songs

Kathryn Kuhlman loved so much; Jimmy McDonald and Irene Oliver sang; and friends, associates, and area pastors participated, each, in his own way, expressing his innermost feelings about this one who will be missed so very, very much.

I had gone to the Los Angeles Shrine service with Jane Jones from Costa Mesa. Jane had been unstinting in hours given to this ministry for ten years. It was difficult for her to comprehend that this would be the last time she'd be driving into Los Angeles to the Shrine for a meeting like this. Jane was representative of the many thousands across the nation who have been involved in Kathryn Kuhlman's ministry. She was gracious and loving. Kathryn knew her well, just as she knew so many others in so many cities and called them her friends. These, too, were co-handmaidens for the Lord. Again, my heart ached for Janie and others like her.

Prior to setting foot in the auditorium I had prayed, "Lord, You've brought me here. You know my time is limited and there are people I really need to see. Arrange it so that I bump into exactly the people you want me to meet. . . ."

Be careful how you pray! God took me at my word and literally had me "bump into" exactly the people He wanted me to see. There was beautiful Sara Hopkins, lovely in green silk. Sara, formerly a Hollywood starlet, in more recent years has co-founded International Orphans, Inc. Sara had received a miraculous healing from cancer. I read her story in Kathryn's book *Nothing Is Impossible With God* and I wondered. I wondered if it would be possible to "bump into" her while in Los Angeles! And there she was, looking beautiful as ever and wonderfully healthy.

I had read about Tom Lewis too in the same book. Tom was called The Latecomer in the chapter about him. I loved his sense of humor, he seemed so transparently honest that I imagined him to be delightful —which he was, for yes, I "bumped into" Tom Lewis!

"Lord, You know I haven't talked to any doctors yet. If possible, it would be awfully nice to meet Dr. Viola Frymann; and oh, yes, that good-looking white-haired doctor we saw a year ago on the platform when we were here. . . ." I was reminding the Lord of just a couple of people I hoped to "bump into."

"Oh, Helen, here's someone you should meet. . . ." It was Jane Jones, tugging at my sleeve. "Dr. Frymann, this is Helen Hosier, she's writing a story about Kathryn. . . ." I looked down into the kindest face wreathed in smiles. We ended up spending the next forty-five minutes in Dr. Frymann's car. It was a most rewarding experience. The personification of graciousness and truth, the doctor told of her many years sitting on the platform at miracle services. "The miracles are real—as real as my sitting here talking to you."

Dr. Frymann is a practicing osteopathic physician and surgeon from La Jolla, California. Had I been a skeptic, my skepticism would surely have evaporated in talking to this woman who attested that the healings were beyond medical explanation.

Shortly after our conversation, upon returning to the Shrine, while walking down a tunnel to my seat, I bumped into the distinguished-looking Dr. Richard Casdorph (whom we'd seen a year before on the platform). Not knowing who he was, however, I stopped him and introduced myself. Just moments before, Dr. Frymann had said to me, "You really must meet Dr. Casdorph. He's been investigating case histories in minute detail of healings. . . ."

I bumped into Paul Ferrin and his daughter Kathy; and Gene Martin, Missionary Director of the Kathryn Kuhlman Foundation. At the service, Gene Martin spoke assuring the audience of the ongoing work of the Foundation and the radio ministry in particular.

But there was someone else whom God intended for me to meet. Jane Jones had mentioned Jean Waltz. "Her ministry with Catholics is really something else," Jane said. "Kathryn was so appreciative of Jean." And would you believe? Yes, we bumped into Jean Waltz next.

It was Jean who provided the title of this very chapter. "We called her ministry 'The Market Place,' " Jean commented upon our introduction.

"Oh, Jean," I responded, "how beautiful! Tell me about your memories of this 'Market Place.' "

"I will," she said. "I'll send them to you." Jean, I discovered a few days later, was a woman of her word. No wonder Kathryn loved *this* handmaiden of the Lord and appreciated her so very much.

I shed some tears in the Shrine that Sunday, March 28, 1976. I wept for Jane Jones, Ruth and Bob Atkins, Dr. Viola Frymann, Sue Birkman, Captain John LeVrier and his wife Sara, Jean Waltz, and the thousands of others who were so close to Kathryn Kuhlman, who loved her, were loyal to her, and who will miss her and the ministry more than mere words can say.

19
"The Book of Acts in Action"

Then Peter, filled with the Holy Spirit, said. . . . "let me clearly state to you and to all the people . . . that it [this healing] was done in the name and power of Jesus from Nazareth, the Messiah, the man you crucified—but God raised back to life again. It is by his authority that this man stands here healed! . . . . There is salvation in no one else! Under all heaven there is no other name for men to call upon to save them."

Acts 4:8, 10, 12

THROUGHOUT HER LIFETIME Kathryn Kuhlman was accused of many things by those who sought to discredit the miracles and the ministry God had entrusted to her. No one, however, could ever accuse her of being prejudiced. It did not matter to her if people were black or white, red or yellow. It was no concern to her whether they were Protestant or Catholic, Jew or agnostic. She had a heart of compassion for everyone.

When Tom Lewis first came to the Shrine service, for instance, in his words, "I saw many Roman-collared men and somberly dressed women, and I wondered what the priests and nuns were doing here." Tom himself was a devout Roman Catholic, later to become numbered in that rapidly growing group who call themselves Catholic Pentecostals.

Tom Lewis was but one of many thousands who came with regularity to the services in various parts of the world. Jean Waltz was another. Jean tells her story like this:

"My mother had just been promoted to heaven and my father did not want to go alone to the Kathryn Kuhlman meeting (at the Shrine), so I attended with him.

"Dr. Charles Price's staff were seated in the front row and they invited me to sit with them. Ruth Fisher of the Kathryn Kuhlman

Foundation office in Pittsburgh came by to visit them and asked if they could suggest someone to help as an 'Advisor' (one who ministers in the aisles during the healing service). They introduced me as I had been active in healing services in America and also in missionary work in Europe. That is how it all began for me . . . which was to last for ten years.

"It was thrilling to see the 'Book of Acts in action.' Although I had been in healing services most of my life I had never seen one like the Kathryn Kuhlman service. It was one of the greatest thrills of my life. All the things I had been taught about healing I had to unlearn in Kathryn's meetings as it was always a new approach. Kathryn had an unusual sense of humor which the audience appreciated. She interviewed each person as if it were the first time she had seen a miracle. She was always excited about the healings and inspired faith. She especially loved the little children and was like a spiritual mother when they were healed.

"She constantly gave all the glory to God for the healings. She knew she was not a 'faith healer.' The minute she walked on the stage she created a beautiful atmosphere of praise and worship. This, too, inspired faith. You could feel the presence of many angels who assisted Kathryn in her meetings. Only God knows the secret and the full impact of her ministry.

"Kathryn was a born organizer. She was like a spiritual general in the Lord's Army. Her ushers were trained, one by one, to handle problems and emergencies. The choir had a special director to prepare them for ministry. Lady Advisors were taught to be led by the Holy Spirit. Workers were assigned to a special area, so all the audience could be ministered to.

"She had a great love for missionary work around the world. . . ."

The Catholic paper *Twin Circle,* November 9, 1975, issue, carried an interview by Vincent J. Ryan, staff writer, with Kathryn Kuhlman. He asked Miss Kuhlman how her relationship with Catholics began. "There was a time in Pittsburgh, years ago, when I was broadcasting over a radio station where the manager Jim Murray was Catholic.

"One day Mr. Murray's parish priest wanted to ask him something: 'Jim,' said the priest, 'who in the world is this Kathryn Kuhlman? For the past three months we have been having more people in our confessional booths confessing that they have been going to see Kathryn Kuhlman. Who in the world is she?' "[45]

Kathryn Kuhlman claimed that at times 60 percent of her audiences were Catholic.

She had a private audience with Pope Paul on October 11, 1972. "When I met Pope Paul there was a oneness. He had an interpreter there, but we needed no interpreter . . . we never used the interpreter. And he did such a beautiful thing. When I walked forward, he recognized me as a person who loves God . . . who had an understanding of the spiritual . . . and he stood and just reached out both hands and took my hand in his and said, 'You're doing an admirable job. You not only have my blessing, you have my prayers.' "[46]

Allen Spraggett, in noting Kathryn Kuhlman's death, in the *Toronto Sun Syndicate* said: "The great secret of Kathryn Kuhlman was her saintlike, universal love for people—regardless of creed, color or caste."

It would have to be agreed that there was a breadth to Kathryn Kuhlman's ministry that can best be described in one word: *Love.*

Jean Waltz was so right when she said Kathryn Kuhlman's ministry was "The Book of Acts in action."

20
Sing, Jerusalem, and Rejoice!

And many nations shall be joined to the Lord in that day,
and shall be my people: and I will dwell in the midst of thee,
and thou shalt know that the LORD of hosts hath sent me
unto thee.

Zechariah 2:11 KJV

A LIFELONG WISH of Kathryn Kuhlman's came true when in 1974 she participated in a World Conference on the Holy Spirit in Jerusalem. The conference attracted international attention drawing together more than 4,500 people from forty different nations; and in excess of 5,000 who crowded every room of Congress Hall on March 3 when Miss Kuhlman conducted a miracle service. It was the largest conference of overseas delegates in modern Israel's history. Later, in describing it, Christian leaders said it was "one of Christendom's most significant meetings in the twentieth century."

Then, once again, in late October and early November 1975, the Second World Conference on the Holy Spirit convened in Jerusalem. This was to be Kathryn Kuhlman's last such gathering, and how significant that it should have taken place in the very city where Jesus spent His last earthly hours.

Wilbur Wacker, pastor of Calvary Church, Torrance, California, and his wife, Shirley, were among the many conferees. Here are his recollections:

"Often you see things better in retrospect than you do in perspective. Perhaps my comments are going to be colored with feeling mainly because Miss Kuhlman's resident physician when she ministered in Los Angeles, is a member in our church. He was aware of Miss Kuhlman's heart condition and told us later that it was only the grace of God and the strength of the Holy Spirit that kept Kathryn Kuhlman on her feet as she ministered in her last months. I didn't know that at the time we were in the audience at the miracle service in Tel Aviv, but we did know she was not feeling too well. We had heard remarks by dear friends and close associates of hers who recognized that her strength was not what it was even a year before at the first conference. A personal friend of mine who was on Miss Kuhlman's staff had told me over a year ago that many felt she seemed to sense the imminent conclusion of her ministry, and rather than slowing down, had even increased their schedule in her deep abiding desire to do all she could.

"My impression of her at the miracle service in Tel Aviv was that she seemed somewhat weary while she was speaking. It was not one of the services that seemed to flow as easily as some—I'm sure there were many reasons for that. For one thing, there were many hundreds of people who had never seen or heard her. Also, there was the language barrier, the problem of translation which always exists in a situation like that.

"But I really believe that the Lord in His own way had shared with her the nearness of her homegoing—perhaps not as dramatically as some people have known this—but an awareness that she lived with. So it was not with too much surprise that as I saw her minister I sensed that she was not strong; I sensed that she was truly holding on to every moment, that there was even more of an urgency in her voice than usual —perhaps more of an urgency within her own self as she reached out to us. When the Holy Spirit began to move in the auditorium, however, she began to be herself again and the anointing seemed to be unusually rich and full.

"Her visage was aglow. Her interest focused more upon people of other nations—when those from the English-speaking world came forward who were healed, she responded graciously, but when people from other nations came, you knew she was even more responsive. As these people were healed, she could hardly contain her rejoicing, especially when that person healed was an Israeli.

"She had one of the soldiers translating for her, and when someone came whose language she did not understand and the Israeli translated, she was just delighted. She seemed to be very comfortable with the Israelis around her.

"Through it all, however, we sensed she was appreciably physically weaker than we'd ever seen her before; yet, she savored *every* moment and *every* incident. It was very beautiful and impressive, and really quite an emotional thing as she called on people from various nations to come and join her as she joined hands with the Israeli soldiers and they formed a line around that huge auditorium."

Shirley Wacker confirmed her husband's observations, and added:

"There were many, many miracles that occurred. But above all, my most cherished memory was the conclusion, as she stood in the center of the stage and asked the soldiers to come and take her hands. Then she asked others representing the other nations to join hands with them. The lines from her went down both sides of the platform, down the stairs, spilling into the aisles and around the auditorium. It was just beautiful! As we stood there with hands clasped together we sang the chorus *"Alleluia,"* the one word universally common. We continued to sing as we left the auditorium and were still singing as we boarded our buses."

Wilbur Wacker related his feelings that as she clasped the hands of those Israelis she may have wondered how many more times she would be standing to minister.

"I really think she had that feeling, because she literally hung on to that service. For the first time since I had been in one of her services (and I've been in many of them), I wanted to leave. It was getting late, but she made no attempt to go. I think it would be entirely correct to say that many people were tired and ready to call it a day. But Miss Kuhlman really wanted to prolong it.

"And that's our last memory of Kathryn Kuhlman—standing on stage, hands lifted, face lifted, singing 'Alleluia!' It was truly precious. Yes, I suppose it is more precious in retrospect than it was even in perspective—we were tourists; we had been traveling; we were weary, but Miss Kuhlman didn't seem to be in a hurry. She was in her element, she was in the Lord's ministry. That's the last time we saw her. We thank the Lord for the memory of her that is so precious, so beautiful. . . ."

Shirley Wacker's concluding thoughts are very meaningful:

"I remember, as we stood there, I thought to myself that this is the way it will be someday when all nations will be gathered together in Israel. Miss Kuhlman seemed to be in that other realm in that moment, perhaps thinking similar thoughts—that in the Presence of Jesus, this is how it will be. . . . In reflection, I wonder if the Lord didn't whisper to her to savor every moment of that foretaste of what was awaiting her."

21

"That Kathryn Kuhlman, She's Quite a Gal!"

*Just think! Though I did nothing to deserve it, and though
I am the most useless Christian there is, yet I was the one
chosen for this special joy of telling the Gentiles the Glad
News of the endless treasures available to them in Christ; and
to explain to everyone that God is the Savior of the Gentiles
too. . . .*

Ephesians 3:8, 9

"WONDERFUL JESUS, I don't have a thing. But if You can take nothing
and use it, I offer You that nothing. I know I love You; all I can give
You is my life and every ounce of strength in my body . . . that's all I
can give. . . ."

Many of the people sitting in the Las Vegas City Auditorium had
doubtless never heard anyone pray like that before. Kathryn Kuhlman
was a different type of attraction!

She came to what is often referred to as Sin City upon the invitation
of the City Council and Mayor Oran Gragson. But it is doubtful
whether she attached that name to Las Vegas any more than she would
have to any other large city in the country. Her response when questioned about the city's reputation was "I hadn't noticed, I've just returned from New York." She could have said Chicago, Los Angeles,
Pittsburgh. She was a gracious lady in every atom of her being.

And Las Vegas loved her!

Eight thousand of the Las Vegas residents and its visitors loved her
—and several thousand others who were left outside of the auditorium
when its seating capacity was exhausted. There were the usual chartered
buses from Reno, Phoenix, Los Angeles, and elsewhere. Chartered

planes flew in from Denver, St. Louis, Dallas, Minneapolis, Seattle, Oakland, and Hawaii. But the Las Vegas populace including casino operators, chorus girls, strippers, prostitutes, gamblers, blackjack dealers, waiters and waitresses, entertainers, and the Christian community sat side by side listening to the woman in white on stage say, "I wouldn't walk across the street to see Kathryn Kuhlman . . . the only reason I stand before you is because of God . . . God loves you . . . it doesn't make any difference to God that this is Las Vegas, so why should it make any difference to me! I don't think Las Vegas has as much sin as Los Angeles and New York. It's just publicized more! I preach the same Gospel here that I preached in St. Louis last week—it is all the power of God."

Her meeting had been well publicized in Las Vegas by those whom one would suspect would be the least likely to welcome her visit to the city—announcements had been made in nightclubs, gambling casinos put up posters. A notice was posted in the dressing room of the largest striptease theatre on the strip. A Jewish comedian, headlining a show at the Circus Maximum, a plush supper club in Caesar's Palace, jabbed his cigar at the packed audience and said, "Oh, by the way, Kathryn Kuhlman's in town. You know who she is, don't you? The mayor has invited her to hold a miracle service in the City Auditorium. . . . I hope you can tear yourselves away from the slot machines to attend. I'll be there. That Kathryn Kuhlman, she's quite a gal!"

His recommendation proved correct.

Local churches had done their part also for weeks prior to her arrival. They worked, prayed, and worked some more. Catholics and Protestants alike joined together to help make "Kathryn Kuhlman Day in Las Vegas" a very special event. The priest at the largest Roman Catholic church conducted a special mass the day before she arrived.

It was definitely a first for the nation's fabled gambling capital. One Las Vegas businessman said although many convention events have been staged in Las Vegas (mostly on behalf of business and industry) no religious undertaking of any such size had been held in the gambling playground. Buses shuttled people back and forth from strip hotels; others walked over from the nearby Hilton, Landmark, Royal Inn, Stardust, and the Sahara.

There were many tears both as Miss Kuhlman spoke and ministered, and as Jimmy McDonald, soloist, sang the old hymns. It was a deeply moving experience to see and hear the magnificent choir of more than 700 voices with full orchestral accompaniment.

As usual, the power of the Holy Spirit fell in a mighty way. Typical of her way of conducting the services, Kathryn called a radiant woman to the stage who had been healed of multiple sclerosis at a miracle service in Los Angeles. Sunny Simons, a chorus girl and wife of a casino operator, told of her healing. Skeptics would prefer to credit Sunny's healing to an acupuncturist or a nutritionist, but Sunny knew better and said so.

Kathryn's message that day has been described as "an old-fashioned Gospel sermon on the Lordship of Christ." Hearers would not soon forget it.

"Nothing is hopeless in the eyes of God," she said. "There is a woman being healed of cancer. Stand up! Claim your healing!"

The audience, accustomed for the most part to the unusual and all that the city offers, gasped as Miss Kuhlman began receiving "words of knowledge" from the Lord concerning healings throughout the vast auditorium.

I wrote to the Las Vegas Strip Chaplain, Jim Reid, with whom I have had correspondence in the past, and asked his help in confirming healings of that day. He so kindly responded by asking the pastor of the Las Vegas First Baptist Church to write and tell me of a remarkable healing. Melvin A. Pekrul, pastor, wrote back:

> "There was a twelve-year-old boy, whose family are members of our church, who walked onto the stage during the healing service claiming healing. The boy's name is Douglas Hall.
>
> "Doug has been afflicted with rheumatoid arthritis for over eight years. His family took him to Mexico about six years ago where he was given a strong medication that alleviated the pain; however, over the years it became apparent that he had stopped growing. He had not grown even a quarter of an inch in the six years.
>
> "They took him to a doctor in Desert Hot Springs, California, who

told them to stop the use of the drug and then put him on a rigorous program of whirlpool baths, stretch exercises, and a special diet. After three months he had gained some weight and he grew a quarter of an inch. However, the sockets in his hips were filling up with calcium causing his knees to come together and making walking difficult. He was confined to bed for a month before the Kuhlman service. He was put in a wheelchair and taken to the service.

"When Kathryn Kuhlman asked those who felt they had been healed to come forward, little Douglas walked up on the stage in full view of the television cameras. When she asked him if he was healed he said that he was.

"His parents report that he has grown *five inches and gained nine pounds* in the months since the healing service. They are elated. He still has some stiffness and eventually surgery will be required to scrape the calcium from the sockets. There definitely came a turning point in his condition, however, as a result of the healing service. The boy continues to make good progress. What a miracle after no growth for five or six years!"

While I was in Los Angeles for the Shrine memorial service for Miss Kuhlman, they showed portions of the film taken that day in Las Vegas. Douglas was moving rapidly back and forth across the platform, his face glowing. Just before leaving Houston, Texas, to fly to the West Coast for that service, I received this letter from the boy's pastor. It was doubly meaningful for me to view that film.

There were other healings. "I would have come to Las Vegas just for the healing of that child," Kathryn Kuhlman said, but there are others who will forever thank and praise the Lord that she came.

Logos Journal in reporting the service said that she stood on her feet ministering for almost five hours, and even then the people continued to come forward.

As usual she made certain of her hearers' salvation.

"Do you want the wonderful assurance of salvation," she asked, her own face wet with tears. "Wouldn't you like to know your sins have been forgiven?" There was no way to hold back the crowd. "Don't come forward unless you are willing to give your heart to Jesus Christ," she pleaded. Thousands packed around the front and down the aisles. Gamblers, chorus girls, the rollers of dice, the rich and the poor rubbed shoulders wanting to be born again. She led them in prayer, 'I confess my sin . . . please cleanse me . . . I give my life to You. . . .' "

When the service was over, the crowd disappeared back into the glittering lights of the strip. But none of the neon signs could outshine the sparkle in the eyes of God's new children, *Logos* reported.

"Las Vegas will probably not change. But many of those in this modern day Pergamos will never be the same. Like Paul in Ephesus, Kathryn Kuhlman had defied Satan in his headquarters."[47]

One can't help but wonder how the Las Vegas Convention Center official felt who reportedly questioned Kathryn Kuhlman prior to the service. "Lady," he said, "did you say this was going to be a religious service? I don't know about the preacher you're bringing in, but whoever it is, he'll never fill it."

Fill it numerically she did, but there was another infilling as well.

A *Las Vegas Sun* account of her service said: "Either it's the greatest show in the world or the Greatest Story Ever Told." I leave it to the reader to drawn his own conclusions as to what happened on that memorable May 3, 1975, in Las Vegas, Nevada!

22
He Touched Me!

. . . Not by might, nor by power, but by my spirit, saith the Lord of hosts.

Zechariah 4:6 KJV

I SHOOK MY HEAD in amazement much of the evening. Imagine, having dinner with a walking miracle! He sat to my left, at the head of the table, where we could all see and listen to him speak. I had read the story of Captain John LeVrier of the Houston Police Department who was miraculously healed of terminal cancer in 1971. And we had seen him at the February 16, 1975, Shrine Auditorium Miracle Service. But now we were sitting by him at the dinner table. He was so vigorous and healthy! A big man, tall and well built with broad shoulders, it seemed incredible that five years before our dinner engagement in March, 1976, he had been near death. Have you ever sat at a table with a walking miracle watching him enjoy a steak?

"She was one of the greatest people of this century. God used her in a tremendous way. I could not say enough kind things about her. All who knew her loved her dearly. I am here today because of Kathryn Kuhlman, but she and I both knew where my healing came from. She always said healing was by the power of God, not by any power of her own.

"Her death came on the fifth anniversary of the day when I met her for the first time in Los Angeles and received my healing from cancer. Three doctors had told me I was going to die, that there was no way I could live; they had never seen a man live who had cancer cells both in the blood stream and in the bone marrow."

Today there are medical specialists who testify that Captain LeVrier's cancer has totally disappeared. Dr. Lowell S. Miller, of the famed M.D. Anderson Hospital and Tumor Institute in Houston, said: "I could not find a single trace of cancer after he visited California. And with the type of cancer he had, there is no spontaneous remission."

Dr. Ardean J. Ediger, a Boise, Idaho, surgeon who documented LeVrier's cure, said that X rays before and after the Kuhlman service showed "he has been unexplainably cured of what was considered incurable cancer."

"Although I have told my story hundreds and hundreds of times since my healing, I enjoy it each time; it feels wonderful to share it," LeVrier said. "I feel like Hezckiah in the Bible who was sick unto death (2 Kings 20:1). God restored him to good health and gave him fifteen more years (*see* v. 6). God didn't tell me how many more years He's going to give me, but I'll tell you one thing, He gave me good health that I'm enjoying! I haven't missed one day's work in over five years due to illness, and haven't taken as much as an aspirin tablet. (I have over a year's sick leave on the books; God has kept sickness away from our door. If I ever feel sick I just pray, 'Lord, keep me well,' and then I say, 'Get away from me, enemy!') When I awaken at night, I just praise Him. There has been continual praise on my lips."

And that's not hard to understand! I'm sure the reader will agree.

Sara LeVrier, the Captain's charming wife, interjected some thoughts that we found meaningful. "All color leaves a cancer victim. John was yellowish-gray when he left for Los Angeles and the Kathryn Kuhlman service. When he came back his cheeks were pink, he had color and strength. He left dragging; he came back and picked up our boys and lifted them up over his head. He hadn't done that for months! I was so awed, but it also frightened me. He kissed me, but I just kind of stayed back away from him, looking at him for days. It was really an awesome thing, but we had to believe it. While it was actually frightening, it *was* real.

"I just didn't know God was that real—that He could take a dead person (and that's what John was) and restore him like that. Well, he's been going strong ever since."

The specter of death is real. "It was so heavy, squeezing us all the time," Sara LeVrier explained.

Someone else who speaks knowingly of what happened is Captain John LeVrier's married daughter, Loraine Geers, wife of a Baptist minister now living in Sikeston, Missouri. "My father's healing was the greatest thing that ever happened in our family. At the time of his illness and the diagnosis of cancer, our whole church joined in praying for him. We especially prayed for him at our Wednesday night prayer meetings." The old Pythian Avenue Baptist Church in Springfield, Missouri, will never be quite the same either, for it was there that Tom Geers pastored at the time.

"My father was the first person I ever knew who was healed like that," Loraine Geers says. "It was the first miracle any of us had ever seen. . . . It showed us that God is really here and working today. Our church was the first place where he gave his testimony in April 1971. He was a living demonstration of the power of the Holy Spirit."

In the years that followed, Kathryn Kuhlman had Captain LeVrier join her in services at such places as McCormick Place in Chicago, in meetings in Minneapolis, Atlanta, Fort Worth, a number of times at the Shrine, Los Angeles, and elsewhere. Wherever he went, he saw miracles take place.

Captain LeVrier has spoken in over a thousand places from 1971 up to 1976, the time this was written. And what kind of a ministry does he have? It should not surprise us that God has chosen to give to this servant whom He counted worthy, a healing ministry. This writer can attest to the humility, the love, the deep sense of awe which is so apparent in this man. There is a godliness about him that radiates the love of Jesus. No wonder Kathryn Kuhlman respected him so very much, and saw him to be another Nathanael, a man of whom Jesus said, "He is without guile, an honest man" (*see* John 1:47).

At the outset of testifying for his Lord, LeVrier asked the Lord a question. "Lord, what do You want me to do? Lord, lead me."

He explains what happened: "God directed me to the Book of James where it says, 'If any of you lack wisdom, let him ask of God, that giveth to all men liberally, and upbraideth not; and it shall be given him. But let him ask in faith, nothing wavering [not doubting] . . .' (1:5, 6).

" 'Lord,' I said, 'if I am to pray for sick people then let me see some get well, then I'll know I'm right where You want me to be.'

"Shortly after that there were three visible healings. Since then there have been many others. Now it's one thing to pray for someone's backache or headache, but it's something else to pray, for instance, for someone in a prayer line where you see a woman shaking so badly with the palsy that you can't even stand to look at her. But she was healed.

"Then there was a mute sixteen-year-old girl in Bethany Baptist Church, Baton Rouge, Louisiana, who had never heard a thing in her life. She was healed.

"The third visible healing was in Scottsdale (Arizona) People's Church at the morning service. A little boy came down the aisle and I got down on my knees to meet him at eye-level. When I asked him what was wrong, he said, 'I can't see out of my left eye.'

"To each of these people I asked the same question: 'Do you believe that Jesus Christ will heal you?' When they said, 'Yes,' I said to them, 'Tonight,' or 'Today,' and each one gave a strong affirmative answer. Then I prayed for each one the same prayer, 'Heal him (or her), Lord Jesus.' When that little fellow came up, I just said, 'Lord, heal him. Heal his left eye,' and I covered up his right eye, the good eye.

"Immediately the little guy jumped up and down shouting, 'I can see, I can see out of my eye!' And you know," LeVrier says, laughing now, "I said, 'Lord, did I have the wrong eye covered up?' That shows you how much faith I had! Later I met a businessman from that same church and he told me the little boy has perfect vision in both eyes!"

Such is the ministry that God has given to one who was healed at a Kathryn Kuhlman meeting in 1971—proof of the fact that it was not by Kathryn Kuhlman's might or power, even as she emphasized over and over again, "But by *my* spirit, saith the Lord of hosts."

Today when the Houston city telephone operators receive a phone call asking for that police officer who has had an unusual thing happen to him, they say, "Yes, just a moment please," and ring for Captain John LeVrier. And when mail comes addressed: To the Policeman Healed of Cancer, Houston, Texas, U.S.A., the postal department knows exactly who should receive the letter!

When *The Houston Post*, Saturday, February 28, 1976, issue carried word of Kathryn Kuhlman's death, they said: "Kathryn Kuhlman once laughingly said that if God could heal a Baptist, He could heal anybody.

"As Kuhlman was buried in California, two Houston Southern Baptists were grieving, yet rejoicing because of their memories of Miss Kuhlman. . . ."

Captain LeVrier said: "Her death is a great loss. We will really miss her."

The Captain stands as representative of the millions who were touched by the Spirit that worked through Kathryn Kuhlman who often said of herself, "I am only an intermediary. . . ."

23
Her Plain Teaching

. . . by our faith—the Holy Spirit helps us with our daily
problems and in our praying. For we don't even know what
we should pray for, nor how to pray as we should; but the Holy
Spirit prays for us with such feeling that it cannot be ex-
pressed in words. And the Father who knows all hearts
knows, of course, what the Spirit is saying as he pleads for
us in harmony with God's own will. And we know that all
that happens to us is working for our good if we love God and
are fitting into his plans.

Romans 8:26–28

KATHRYN KUHLMAN was named after one of her great-grandmothers.
Someone else in the family didn't want her named *Kathryn* because
"Every mule in Missouri is called *Kate.*"

Some will call it stubbornness; others will say it was persistence.
Stubborn or persistent, Kathryn herself was too busy seeking to learn all
she could from the Word of God, and too busy doing what she understood to be the will of God, to bother about terms. If she was somewhat
mulish, so be it.

"The Holy Spirit gives boldness," she said to us in February, 1975.
"We don't even have to ask Him for it. It just comes with the Holy
Spirit. I could never tell you the boldness the Holy Spirit gives me, and
it's not Kathryn Kuhlman."

When the early apostles were speaking with such boldness and courage in Jerusalem after the descent of the Holy Spirit upon them, the
religious council convened. They were greatly disturbed because "a
notable and tremendous miracle had been done" by Peter and John. The
two were imprisoned and then brought in and questioned. Peter's explanation was simple: "Let me clearly state to you and all the people of

Israel that it was done in the name and power of Jesus of Nazareth, the Messiah, the man you crucified—but God raised him back to life again."[48]

Kathryn Kuhlman's words were an echo of the early apostles.

She was often asked, "Miss Kuhlman, how is one 'filled' with the Holy Spirit?"

"It's so simple," she said in reply. "So simple that most folks miss it. 'He is with you,' the Scripture says, 'but He shall be in you.' If you are born again the Holy Spirit is with you. It is the Holy Spirit that convicts us of sin—know that—the Holy Spirit is a mighty convicting power.

"But when the slaying power of the Holy Spirit comes upon you— there are those who witness to the fact that it's like a bolt of electricity, but you are dealing with something greater in you than electricity— these physical bodies of ours can take just so much, they are not geared for all this power, do you understand?

"When He comes in, it is as you worship and adore Jesus, for Jesus said, 'He (the Holy Spirit) would magnify Me,' and you get exactly what you seek.

"Many a person has sought tongues—you cannot show to me from the Word of God that you and I were ever commanded to seek tongues (and I believe in speaking in an unknown tongue; I believe in it with every atom of my being; it's in the Bible and I've got to believe it), but in the house of Cornelius (when Peter was speaking, Acts 10:44) they were listening intently when 'the Holy Spirit fell upon all those listening!'

"And in the Upper Room where the 120 were present (*see* Acts 1), they were waiting for the Holy Spirit to come upon them in fulfillment of the Father's promise (*see* Acts 1:4). They were seeking Him, the Holy Spirit, and in the final analysis, my friend, when you talk about the Baptism of the Holy Spirit it's still *just more Jesus and more and more and more of Jesus.*

"And what is speaking in an unknown tongue if you don't have the power of the Holy Ghost and the love of Jesus? If you get down on your knees and pray for tongues, you're not scriptural. But if you seek more of Jesus and the Holy Spirit comes in through praying and adoration and you worship Jesus, 'You will glorify Me,' He said. When you get to the place that you love Jesus with all of your heart, then it's so easy to die to self and it isn't a matter of struggling. Then when you are completely surrendered the Holy Spirit comes in and He will announce His own incoming, and it isn't that you seek evidence. *The evidence will come* —you don't have to ask for the evidence—you don't seek the evidence. There will be power in your life, for Jesus Himself said, 'Ye shall receive power, after that the Holy Ghost is come upon you . . .' (Acts 1:8 KJV).

"Don't put words in the mouth of Jesus," she cautioned. "Don't go contrary to the teaching of the Master—He knows human nature so well. The greatest evidence of having been filled with the Holy Spirit will be fruits of the Spirit.

"Read 1 Corinthians 13. If you really want to know if someone has been filled up with the Holy Spirit there will be evidence of fruit—'Love suffereth long, and is kind; love envieth not; love is not puffed up.' Does your experience measure up with this? You do not have the fruits of the Spirit if you have spiritual pride—when you say, 'I have been filled with the Spirit and I've got the Baptism of the Holy Spirit, I have all the gifts of the Spirit. . . .' The more you talk, the more puffed up you get, and I feel like taking a pin and puncturing the balloon. I want to get away from someone like that so fast. One of the greatest Christian graces is humility. And if you have received the Baptism of the Holy Spirit, remember, one of the fruits is *humility*. When it comes to not only the fruits, but the gifts of the Spirit—you're not going to boast of it, you're not going to talk about it.

"These things are so sacred; like a beautiful jewel; they are precious. No one will ever hear Kathryn Kuhlman boast that she has been given any gifts of the Holy Spirit. . . . There is a responsibility that goes with receiving a gift, and you guard it so carefully, and He gives you a reward in what the Holy Spirit has done and has given you. I beg of you," she pleaded, "if you are boasting about the gifts of the Spirit, be careful, very careful . . . it's a sacred trust, something so precious you don't go around talking about it."

When it came to the actual matter of speaking in tongues she was very explicit in stating her beliefs. "When the Holy Spirit does the speaking," she emphasized, "He speaks perfectly and it's going to be beautiful. Sometimes in the actions of some people, you almost get the idea that the Holy Spirit is an imbecile. He's not an imbecile! The One through whom Jesus offered Himself to the Spirit was perfect wisdom, perfect knowledge, perfect in all things. And when He speaks, He speaks beautifully.

"You do not have to seek the manifestation, you just surrender to Him, and when you do, He does the rest."

She referred people to Romans 8:26–28. When this happened to her she was very young, she said. But she always remembered the advice of a dear old gentleman who took her hand in his and cautioned, "Never get out of the will of God, girl." She didn't exactly know for certain what he was talking about, "but I know now," she added. "Yes, I know now, my own nature is to be impulsive." But she heeded the advice and God honored her ministry.

"When I died to self, when I gave Him body, soul and spirit, He came in and He spoke," she said. "It was so deeply moving."

Kathryn saw her own mother have the experience of speaking in a heavenly language. "Mama never knew there was such a thing; she'd never heard it; she had no light on it; and she wasn't seeking for it. Explain these things? Who can! It was glorious. I have to believe in an unknown tongue; I have no choice. When Mama opened her eyes she took my hands in hers, and it was the first time that she had ever approved of me being in this work. She said, 'Kathryn, preach that others may have what I have received.' " She related that her mother did not sleep for three days and two nights, so great was her joy in the Lord. "I had a new mama. Love radiated from her. Nobody had to prompt her; nobody had to teach her. But oh, the joy; oh, the love. Mama was never the same!"

She emphasized that she wouldn't want to be out of the will of God for anything in the world. "Remember, when you get to the place where you have no will of your own then you can't miss the will of God! What an easy place to get to!"

Her teaching on the matter was firm. "Remember something else: the Holy Spirit is not given for our own pleasure and our own enjoyment.

The Holy Spirit is given for service. You are misusing the Holy Spirit, you are misusing this wonderful Person, if you are using Him for your own pleasure—a little 'spiritual picnic' when you get together with some of the 'saints of God.' You are misappropriating the Power of the Holy Spirit when you act like that. But there is a time when you know not how to pray, but there is One who knows the perfect will of God, and He never works separate and apart from the Father or separate and apart from Jesus . . . He has perfect knowledge as to the will of God, and when I get to the place where I have no will of my own, and throw myself upon this Person who dwells *within*, then He comes before the throne and makes intercession for me, and He speaks for me. In this way I can never miss the will of God, for He knows His will and talks to the Father for me."

24
"I Believe in Miracles"

*Stephen, the man so full of faith and the Holy Spirit's power,
did spectacular miracles among the people.*

Acts 6:8

"TELEVISION BECAME her medium." It was Dick Ross speaking. Dick
Ross, known and highly respected in the television and motion picture
industry, the man behind the beautifully produced and directed television program "I Believe in Miracles," a man Kathryn Kuhlman dearly
loved and for whom she had great respect and admiration. "Even though
she was one of my clients, we were very good friends as well," he stated.
"We used to meet every other month for about three hours on Mondays
for breakfast preceding the Wednesday and Thursday taping schedule
at CBS."

It was a marvelous opportunity for Kathryn Kuhlman to "let her hair
down," in the presence of someone she knew could keep a confidence.
"I always felt that our relationship was God-ordained," Ross commented. "It began right at the time when I'd left the Billy Graham
organization (after being with them fourteen years), and when I was
trying to reassess what direction my career should go on an independent
basis."

They met at the Century Plaza Hotel in Century City, where she
always stayed. "She was thinking of televising her miracle services and
I strongly advised against it and, instead, came up with the program
format which, for the most part, remained the same all these years."

Her television program was the longest running half-hour series that
CBS ever had. "We did just under five hundred shows in just under ten
years," Dick Ross explained. "Kathryn didn't believe in reruns. She
didn't want to give people the idea that God wasn't doing anything new,
anything fresh. We went to reruns sparingly and then only when her

schedule became so crowded she couldn't work in taping sessions.

"Her style on radio was reminiscent of the 1930s. It was an old-fashioned style, the 'Are you waiting for me?' thing, but on television she rose to the professional standard which is so necessary if a program is to gain audience approval. She still had a style of interviewing that many people had difficulty getting accustomed to, but she did extremely well considering the fact that she actually was a nonprofessional."

Did Kathryn Kuhlman take suggestions easily from a professional such as Dick Ross? "Indeed she did. I could make a suggestion about the content of a two or three minute opening, and she'd just nod her head and go ahead and do it. She was just magnificent! There is only one other person that I've worked with in the religious field who had that ability."

She was herself greatly admired and respected by the television and movie professionals. "They would have detected her nonprofessional hang-ups instantly because that's their business. I know many professional people who just took to her immediately and were so attracted to her. She had an ability of meeting people from show business—highly successful people—and not being awed by them; therefore, she had a rapport with them on a one-to-one basis. I was impressed with the way she handled them—and more important—was of help to them. There are many in this profession who are alive today because of God's use of Kathryn Kuhlman as His instrument. These are individuals of enormous capabilities. Right from the start Kathryn Kuhlman was accepted by the CBS staff and became sort of a queen of the lot. When she'd come into the studio there was a constant procession of people from the executive level on down—people who loved her—who would stop by just to see her and say hello.

"She really won the confidence of the entire West Coast CBS operation. If there was a problem of any kind, they would break their necks just because they adored her. She ministered to many of them on a personal level both in a physical (healing) way as well as on the spiritual level. In many instances, where there were problem areas in their lives, she would take a few moments in the course of her busy work day at the studio to help them.

"One of the finest costume designers in the industry came to Kathryn one day, and Kathryn made a great impact spiritually on this woman. After that, many of the clothes that were so stunning which Kathryn wore were designed by this woman."

Kathryn's television wardrobe was always in the best of taste, it is generally agreed. The word *class* has been used elsewhere in this book to describe Kathryn Kuhlman's preferences in regard to certain aspects of her personal life, but the same word can be used with regard to all that she did for the Lord. Whatever she did she wanted it to be right, *first class* for the One who had done so much for her.

"The garden setting which we gradually evolved was geared to her personality and love for flowers," Dick Ross explained. "The very competent people with whom we worked on the network were always eager to see to it that she got what she needed and wanted. But she was so easy to work with, it was always a pleasure to please her. She took suggestions and directions very well. More than anybody I've ever worked with, she had the ability to articulate standard introductions or interviews, or a message with a minimum of preparation. The reason? Because she was so full of her subject that verbalizing it was second nature to her."

Dick Ross was saying, in effect, that Kathryn Kuhlman lived what she preached. She lived what she taught. "There was nothing planned about her actions. It was not a technique that she developed just in front of the TV camera—nothing of that nature. When she did what she called a heart-to-heart talk—this was a short fifteen to eighteen minute meditation—her repetition and her *ex-ag-ger-ated* syllable for syllable way of speaking was just her. But it's also recognized as a very good teaching technique. There are people who deliberately do that to drive it into your mind and they will hit it from different positions saying the same thing in different ways. But when Kathryn was doing those kinds of messages, it was just her and most effective. In spite of those exaggerated mannerisms, it really 'paid off' in terms of effectiveness."

I learned that Kathryn Kuhlman never rehearsed her programs. Many of the people who appeared as her guests she had never met before. Often she learned of their remarkable miracle healing through correspondence. Others might have appeared on the platform at some miracle service, but then only briefly. When letters arrived telling of a remarkable healing, Maggie would research, verify, and do the followup. Only after thorough investigation were individuals invited to appear on television programs. Many of these individuals were healed at a Shrine (Los Angeles) service; still others at the First Presbyterian Church services in Pittsburgh; and some from Youngstown services and from other cities. "It's amazing the cross section of humanity who were touched by her ministry," Dick Ross said, "and I only met the ones on TV, and for every one of those there were scores of others with equally dramatic stories and miracle healings."

Kathryn Kuhlman, it was obvious from her television programs, possessed a flair for the unusual. "She always wanted to do things that had not been done before," her television producer and director emphasized, as he continued:

"The Las Vegas Special—the ninety-minute film of the meeting in Las Vegas—was really Kathryn's idea. It was the best thing I've ever done with her. In all the years we worked together we had an agreement that cameras would not be used during a miracle service. The first time it was done, it was almost without her full consent in Jerusalem. Perhaps God in His wisdom knew Kathryn had less than a year to live and burdened her to preserve one miracle service as a testimony for posterity. But the Las Vegas Special was her idea and a tremendous one.

"Kathryn was an innovator. But, never to my knowledge, did she take advantage of the fact that there were many celebrities whom she knew who came to see her. She would say to me, 'Dick, what could they have to say on the program? They are people who are seeking. I can't do an interview with someone who is seeking, just because they have a name.' And I think she is to be admired for that quality. She was not an opportunist. She never took advantage of people and she surely could have."

Did she and Dick Ross have differences? "We had some battles over the budget. She carried a heavy load of responsibility businesswise; she made all the decisions. So I worked with her directly on these matters also. But she was a great one for wanting things done right. She wanted things done first-class for the Lord, as I've already indicated, and that desire would enable me to at least do things to a fair degree of technical excellence." Dick went on to explain:

"Kathryn had another quality that great stars have. There were many times when she'd come into the studio very tired, but in just a moment of time she could go from complete letdown and an out-of-the-mood feeling to being up for the rolling of tape or cameras or whatever the medium.

"The last eight shows she made probably hastened her hospitalization during Christmas week (1975). I don't think anyone who knew her intimately could tell that she was ill by watching her before the cameras during those last programs. Every day that we taped we would always go down to the screening room afterwards and do what we called a quality control check. We would spotcheck all of the shows and she would have an opportunity to see herself. She would invite the guests to stay and see five or six minutes of their interview just as a little gesture of appreciation. But I remember the last show we made—the last four —I went with her to the dressing room and she just didn't make it. The room had a flight of stairs, about four steps up from the dressing room where we did the screening, and there was a chair at the foot of the stairs and she said, 'Just let me sit here, I'm really tired . . . I'm just bushed.' She looked up at me and for the first time in ten years she said, 'Dick, will you scrub the screening of the shows,' and she meant by that "Will you cancel my screening them this time?" It was not only her habit to see them, but she also enjoyed it. So we knew she was really ill.

"Tink Wilkerson took her to the hotel and ultimately to a local hospital where she stayed before going on to Pittsburgh, and on to Tulsa (to the hospital).

"Everyone in the organization knew that she had some kind of heart aberration for years. Maggie told me about it, that when she overdid that she would just have to stop and recoup. Nevertheless, her death was a great blow. . . ."

What general observations did Dick Ross have as to Kathryn Kuhlman's ministry after so closely observing and working with her for a decade?

"First, I noticed that the great majority of people healed made no pretense of being Christians. Many had been involved in cults; others were highly skeptical, and some even had no belief in God. But God seemed to thrust Himself upon them in such a way that there was no denying Him or His power. But the pattern was never the same. You can't put God in a box and especially was this true with Kathryn Kuhlman's ministry.

"Then I discovered that when people had a bona-fide healing, this was always accompanied by a spiritual experience. I think, for instance, of my friend Captain John LeVrier. John was a nominal kind of Christian, but this healing revolutionized his spiritual as well as his physical life. He is but one such example; there are literally many hundreds of others.

"Third, these people never forget their healing experience. It is always as fresh as if it happened yesterday!

"And finally, God seems to have singled out people for this experience that He knows will have an influence on others in some area or areas. The influence factor is strong, they are faithful in their witness."

We discussed the fact that all of this was in harmony with divine order and the clear teachings of the Word of God. Kathryn Kuhlman was not unlike Stephen in the Book of Acts. Stephen was described as a man full of faith and the Holy Spirit's power—a man whose face became as radiant as an angel's—and who did spectacular miracles among the people (*see* Acts 6). The description fits Kathryn Kuhlman.

"Yes," Dick Ross said as we concluded our time together, "television became her medium. It went hand in glove with her platform services. The platform services were where the miracles happened; the television series became the means of sharing with millions across the country."

Who can ever forget this woman whose television ministry was a constant affirmation, "I be . . . leeva in miracles!"

25
The Legacy She Left

No man can live forever. All will die. . . .

Psalms 89:48

"Now SHE HAS her questions answered!"

More than one person made that comment upon learning of Kathryn Kuhlman's death.

The two questions that were asked of her more frequently than any others had to do with what she called "coming under the power" and the question relating to "Why wasn't everyone healed?"

In talking to her in February, 1975, she said: "I call it 'coming under the power' when people fall backwards, because I do not know what else to call it. I only know that I have nothing to do with it. One of the questions I'm going to ask the Master when I get home to glory is this manifestation of His power, the 'slaying power' of the Holy Spirit. I do not understand it. There is a biblical criterion for it, however, I feel."

She was referring to the conversion of Saul, later to be called the Apostle Paul, on the Damascus road in Acts 9; also mention of this manifestation is made in the Gospels (*see* John 18:4–6 and Matthew 17:6).

"I'm sure that even Paul didn't understand it. If he had, we can be almost certain he would have explained it. But he did have that unusual experience and because he did not understand, and God did not reveal it to him, he left it there, and I think we should too," she said.

In answer to the question, "Why isn't everyone healed?" she said: "I don't know why someone who has prayed so earnestly for a healing wasn't healed . . . I just don't know. You have no idea how much I want an answer to that.

"Why isn't everyone healed?" she repeated the question, and you could feel the great ache in her heart as she said it. "I thrill to the healing of these sick bodies. The last healing I saw is as thrilling as the first. No one is more thrilled than I am when I look at a little Lisa and a leg that *was* to be amputated and is now whole. I had nothing to do with it. *It was God!*

"At the close of a service I feel so . . . ." and she fumbled for the right word, ". . . so *repaid*. Y' know what I mean, don't ya?"

Yes, we knew. Not from firsthand experience as she did, but we understood what she was saying by the way she said it—hands outstretched imploringly, bending over, head tilted in a characteristic gesture, eyes pleading. "But I tell you honestly, I can hardly stand it when I pass on the street those who are still being pushed in their wheelchairs. No, I don't have God's perfect wisdom and perfect knowledge; but even as the wheelchairs are being pushed out, I often see a smile that may not have been there before. If through the lifting up of Jesus, if in telling how big God is, I can give hope, then I had rather not be known as the lady of faith . . . but the lady who gives hope; the lady who puts windows in blank walls; the lady who puts doors where there were no doors; the lady who inspires confidence.

"One miracle everyone can experience is the spiritual . . . the new birth experience. That is the greatest miracle of all.

"The more I learn of Jesus, and the closer my walk with Him, I realize how little I really know.

"Do you really want to know what Jesus is like? Go through the deep waters in the night that is so dark there isn't a star in the sky and you will realize He is there!

"When you come to the edge of *your* Red Sea and there is no way forward or back, He will part the waters for you.

"But why wasn't everyone healed at those great services? I would never say it is because of lack of faith. I don't believe that. I'm not quite sure I know altogether what faith is, although I've often tried explaining it. But I do know a little of the mercy of the Lord Jesus Christ. I know a little of the love of God. I know a little of the glorious power of the Holy Spirit, and I would not want to live if I did not have that fellowship with the Holy Spirit. I only know that miracles do take place—not because of a person's goodness—not because someone has earned it—

not because they've deserved it—but it is all of mercy.

"I just have to trust a God who is perfect wisdom and perfect knowledge.

"But, oh, what I *can* tell you is the wonderful fellowship and the power of the Holy Spirit. All these things can belong to anyone, even though there may not be a miraculous healing."

She paused that day in the Shrine Auditorium dressing room. She hadn't meant to preach a sermon, but she just had. She realized it, and with a twinkle in her eyes, she clasped her hands, shook her head and smiled, "God is so good, so-o-o-o merciful," and we nodded our heads in silent agreement. It was an emotional moment.

But now that voice—so often choked with emotion—is silent.

She was first hospitalized in Tulsa, Oklahoma, in the summer of 1975 and in Los Angeles, California, in November and December for what were described as "minor heart flare-ups." Then, through the ministrations of "Tinker" Wilkerson, a Tulsa friend, she was admitted to the Hillcrest Medical Center in Tulsa again on December 27 and underwent surgery to replace a heart valve and repair a tendon. She recovered from the surgery, but newspapers reported Mr. Wilkerson as stating that "she failed to regain her strength."

Shock waves of grief and disbelief went around the world when news of her death was reported Friday, February 20, 1976. Perhaps David Vercilli (Youngstown, Ohio) described it best at the memorial service held for her in Stambaugh Auditorium: "It was absolutely one of the most unbelievable things of my life . . . when I heard it I was stunned. Something went out of me . . . a void that must be filled by God Himself."

Memorial services were held throughout the nation to honor the memory of this one who served the Lord so faithfully for well over fifty years. "We loved her dearly; God loved her best," Vercilli said. Then he asked the question that lay heavy upon the hearts of mourners the world over: "What are we going to do without our preacher lady?"

Private funeral rites for 150 invited friends were held at Forest Lawn Memorial Park in Glendale, California, on February 24. Honorary pallbearers included the Rev. Rex Humbard (Ohio pastor and evangelist), the Rev. Ralph Wilkerson (Melodyland Christian Center pastor, Anaheim, California), and the Rev. Leroy Sanders (pastor of North Hollywood First Assembly of God, Hollywood, California).

At the service Dr. Oral Roberts spoke stating, "To me she's the greatest evangelist of the ministry of God's miracle power in my lifetime. . . . I feel very strongly that in her death a great many people will be touched."

The Rev. Ralph Wilkerson, in tribute to her memory, said, "The spirit that was in Kathryn walked with God."

Dan Malachuk, writing in the *National Courier* commented: "There are thousands who will rise on that great day and bless God for Kathryn Kuhlman and her demonstration of Christian charity and devotion to the Lord of Lords, Jesus Christ."[49]

David Wilkerson remarked: "Without a shadow of a doubt, this was a great woman of God. She was a classic example of an encouragement to anyone who wants to be used of the Lord. God doesn't use angels; He uses people with all of their weaknesses and strengths. He used Kathryn Kuhlman mightily."

Her Concordia neighbor and friend, Roland Petering, wrote:

I enjoyed Kathryn's telecasts as well as her books, but I have reason to believe that no one could truly appreciate the magnitude or quality of her ministry unless they had actually attended one of her services. Being an old hardboiled business man and retired naval officer, I thought I had seen a lot of the world and had been exposed to many people and their beliefs. Frankly, I attended Kathryn's miracle service in Kansas City out of friendship as well as curiosity. I must admit that through her ministry and the way the service was conducted, I felt the Presence of Someone Unseen which I couldn't quite explain. I wondered about it for many months and it wasn't until a week before her untimely demise that I finally realized why so many people had expressed the same feeling.

Although I have attended church regularly all my life, I must say in all candor that during that miracle service I really felt the Presence of the Holy Spirit. That, I believe, explains to my satisfaction why she had such a large following of people, some of whom experienced physical as well as spiritual healings.

I think Kathryn Kuhlman herself would have been deeply moved by these words from her childhood friend.

Ruth Atkins (Akron, Ohio), longtime devoted friend and co-worker shared that Kathryn's dying words were: "Love . . . love . . . love." Ruth said, "She often reminded us of the Apostle Paul's words: 'And now abideth faith, hope, [love], these three; but the greatest of these is [love]' (1 Corinthians 13:13). Kathryn told us in heaven all we'd need would be love. . . ."

When word came through from UPI (United Press International) and appeared in the late news on Saturday, March 27, 1976 (one month and seven days following her death), regarding the dispersion of Kathryn Kuhlman's estate, my own reaction was that the real legacy she left could never be measured in terms of dollar value.

"The present-day Church," she said, "needs to get to the place where we will quit limiting the ministry of the Holy Spirit, and begin to pray and believe God for the enriching and enlarged ministry of the Third Person in His blessed fullness. All this is tied together, intertwined throughout the Word and in the experiences of His Own.

"Jesus meant the Holy Spirit to be as Himself among us until the very ending of the age. And the touch of the Lord is the moving of the Holy Spirit in us, through us, and for us."

I wonder if, when Kathryn Kuhlman stepped across the threshold dividing earth and heaven, Jesus gently took her by the hand. Leading her around heaven, presenting her at the throne of the Father, and in introducing her, He may have said: "I know she needs no introduction, but this is Kathryn—Kathryn Kuhlman, Your handmaiden. She carried a water bucket for Us."

About a month and a half after Kathryn Kuhlman's death, another figure who had been prominently featured in the world's news for many years also died. In Las Vegas, Nevada, a television announcer was talking to a man in one of the Casinos. The man said, "Isn't it a shame that Howard Hughes had to die to prove that he was alive?"

That will never have to be said of Kathryn Kuhlman!

David Vercilli said of her that "her life was epitomized by the fact that she gave and she gave and she gave—and that was indicative of a heart full of life and love."

The legacy she left? Who can adequately measure or describe it? In the front of Loraine Geer's Bible she wrote: "May the Lord keep you in His tender care always! Love, KATHRYN KUHLMAN." And that, I believe, is what she would have said to each reader if she could have had one final word with you.

When David Wilkerson wrote this in the Foreword of her book *Nothing Is Impossible With God,* she was moved. It stands as the finest final tribute one can pay to a woman of this stature:

History will say of Kathryn Kuhlman

Her living and her dying
Brought glory to God.

Source Notes

Chapter 1

1 1 Corinthians 1:27 KJV.
2 Matthew 7:1 KJV.
3 John 5:30 KJV.
4 Psalms 9:8 KJV.
5 1 Corinthians 2:14 KJV.

Chapter 2

6 Allen Spraggett, *Kathryn Kuhlman: The Woman Who Believes in Miracles* (Cleveland, Ohio: The World Publishing Company, 1970), p. 173.
7 "Kathryn Kuhlman Superstar," *Pittsburgh Press,* February 3, 1974, p. 19.

Chapter 3

8 Much of the information in this chapter was gleaned from a series of articles written by W.F. Walkenhorst, Kathryn Kuhlman's grandfather, for the *Concordian,* the local weekly newspaper published in Concordia, Missouri. The articles were written in 1925, 1926, and 1927.
9 Additional information for this chapter comes from the book *Concordia, Missouri: A Centennial History* by Harry R. Voight, 1960 Centennial Committee, Concordia, Missouri. Used by permission.

Chapter 4

10 Matthew 10:12–14 KJV.

Chapter 6

11 "Miracle Woman," *Time* magazine, September 14, 1970, p. 62.
12 Dan L. Thrapp, "Preacher Sways Throngs With Healing Services," *Los Angeles Times,* February 19, 1970, p. 1.
13 "Healing in the Spirit," *Christianity Today,* July 20, 1973, p. 5.
14 Acts 2:17,18 KJV.

Chapter 7

15 Catherine Nixon Cooke, "The Business of Making Miracles," *Coronet* magazine, December, 1974, p. 34.

Chapter 8

16 "Truly a Worker of God," *National Courier*, March 19, 1976, p. 5.
17 "No Second Miss Kuhlman Apparent," *Los Angeles Times*, March 1, 1976, pp. 1,3.
18 Allen Spraggett, *Kathryn Kuhlman: The Woman Who Believes in Miracles* (Cleveland, Ohio: The World Publishing Company, 1970), p. 135.
19 *Ibid.*, p. 127.

Chapter 10

20 Kathryn Kuhlman, *I Believe in Miracles* (Old Tappan, New Jersey: Spire Books, 1969), p. 213.
21 *Los Angeles Times*, September 12, 1965.
22 Kuhlman, *I Believe in Miracles*, p. 215.

Chapter 11

23 *See* Romans 8:11.

Chapter 12

24 Allen Spraggett, *Kathryn Kuhlman: The Woman Who Believes in Miracles* (Cleveland, Ohio: The World Publishing Company, 1970), pp. 161, 162.
25 *Ibid.*, 162,163.

Chapter 13

26 Ecclesiastes 1:2 KJV.
27 Catherine Nixon Cooke, "The Difficult Business of Making Miracles," *Coronet* magazine, December 12, 1974, p. 34.
28 "Kathryn Kuhlman Superstar," "Roto," February 3, 1974, p. 21.

Chapter 14

29 "Kathryn Kuhlman: Dying to Self," *Christianity Today*, p. 47.
30 *Ibid.*
31 Romans 9:15,16 KJV.

Chapter 15

32 "Truly a Worker of God," *National Courier*, March 19, 1976, p. 26.

Chapter 16

33   Allen Spraggett, *Kathryn Kuhlman: The Woman Who Believes in Miracles*
     (Cleveland, Ohio: The World Publishing Company, 1970), p. 134.
34   Dan L. Thrapp, "Preacher Sways Throngs With Healing Services," *Los
     Angeles Times,* February 19, 1970, p. 1.
35   "Healing in the Spirit," July 20, 1973, p.5.
36   Kathryn Kuhlman, *I Believe in Miracles* (Old Tappan, New Jersey: Spire
     Books, 1969).
37   *Ibid.*
38   *See* Luke 8:43–48; Mark 5:25–34; Matthew 9:20–22.
39   Kuhlman, *I Believe in Miracles,* p. 128.

Chapter 17

40   2 Corinthians 11:27.
41   Acts 1:8 KJV.

Chapter 18

42   John 16:7 KJV.
43   John 16:17,18.
44   John 16:13,14.

Chapter 19

45   Vincent J. Ryan, "Kathryn Kuhlman—A Look at the Minister as Healer,"
     Twin Circle, November 9, 1975.
46   *Ibid.*

Chapter 21

47   "Kathryn Kuhlman in Las Vegas," *Logos Journal,* July-August, 1975, pp.
     33–36.

Chapter 23

48   Acts 4:10

Chapter 25

49   "Kathryn Kuhlman: God's Servant," *National Courier,* March 18, 1976,
     p. 26.